For Peter, to remind Yo [barcode] W9-CFB-557
Wedding day up north in ♡

Love
Cathy (mother-in-law)

Quiet Magic

Quiet Magic
Sam Cook

Illustrations by Bob Cary

 Pfeifer-Hamilton

Grateful acknowledgment is made to the *Duluth News-Tribune* for permission to reprint these stories and columns, which originally appeared in that newspaper.

Pfeifer-Hamilton
210 West Michigan Duluth MN 55802-1908
218-727-0500

Quiet Magic

Printed in the United States of America

10 9 8 7 6 5 4 3

Book design by Barbara Pederson, Minneapolis MN.

Library of Congress Cataloging in Publication Data
88-062599

ISBN 0-938586-17-3

For Emily

Acknowledgments

There would have been no Quiet Magic, nor stories for it, without the support and understanding of Phyllis, my wife. Together we made the compromises that permitted so many of my trips and still kept some sense and order in our lives. I thank her not only for doing what needed to be done in my absence, but for knowing why I needed to go in the first place.

I also express my continuing appreciation to the Duluth News-Tribune, with whose permission this collection of stories and essays is published. Most of the pieces first appeared as part of my weekly writing for that newspaper. I am most grateful to its management for the freedom given me to pursue stories and to express my feelings. After eight years it's still fun.

I am indebted to Don Tubesing and the whole staff at Pfeifer-Hamilton, first for wanting to do this book, and second, for making it an enjoyable process. Larry Fortner, my editor at Pfeifer-Hamilton, knows how to handle not only an editor's pencil but a canoe paddle and Duluth pack as well. That made his suggestions and critique doubly valuable.

Now I need to back up a few years and thank someone who probably thinks I've forgotten her. Anne Wognum, publisher of the Ely Echo weekly newspaper in Ely, Minnesota, gave me my first opportunity to write for a newspaper. Everyone has to start somewhere, and I will always have a fondness for that little office on the corner of Sheridan Street and Central Avenue in Ely.

Along the way in any writer's career — if you're lucky — someone who knows what writing is about takes you aside, roughs up your copy and teaches you the little things that make a difference. For me those people were Lee Spaulding and Brad Hurd, with whom I crossed paths in Longmont, Colorado. They took a lot of bad habits out of me and put a lot of good ones in their place. And they did it gently, which was nice.

Finally, I am grateful to all of the people in these stories who let me paddle and ski and camp with them, who let me describe for the world the shapes of their bodies and the cut of their faces, and who shared with me places of significance in their lives. Some of you called to suggest a story and quite innocently became part of one. Others allowed me to intrude at my request for a couple of hours or a couple of days. Still others are old friends who might have preferred not to be held up for public scrutiny, but who went along with it anyway. I am richer for having traveled with all of you.

S. C.
Duluth, Minnesota

Contents

Spring

Summer

Fall

Winter

Quiet Magic

It would be easy, in this country Up North, to let the little things slip by. When you live in a place that gives you bull moose and Northern Lights, it is possible to overlook the little moments and the small sightings that sweeten the passing of time between larger events.

I remember savoring a sunset from a campsite on Disappointment Lake in the canoe country out of Ely, Minnesota. It was one of those glorious celebrations of light, an explosion of sky and color and clouds set off against still water and a distant saw-toothed ridge.

Finally, I thought the show was over. The sun was down. The reds and blues and purples had begun to pale. Then I looked down at my feet. In the water, not more than a paddle's length from shore, was a stand of reeds — some leaning, some folded back on themselves and dangling in the water. They were silhouetted against flat water that reflected the sunset's lingering pastels.

As splendid as the sunset had been, what remains most vivid to me through the years is the simplicity of those reeds, stark against the peach backdrop. I had found the Quiet Magic. It was right in front of me.

Spring

Lures and Lust

I walk through the door and say hello to the store owner. He knows me. He probably has a good idea what I'm up to.

It is a noon hour in spring. I have come to lust. He can see it in my eyes. He has seen my kind before: preoccupied, a little desperate. That is why we come to his sporting goods store in the spring.

A friend of mine is on his way out. He has just bought his wife a plane ticket to Florida, he says. Feeling somewhat magnanimous about that, he thought maybe he'd just look at the fish locators — the Humminbirds and Eagles and all the rest. The little electronic boxes that tell you everything you want to know: what the lake bottom looks like and where the fish are that won't bite.

My friend says he has an old Lowrance depth finder, the one called a "green box" by anglers. Works fine, he says, but he was looking at these new $300 to $500 gizmos just the same. Because he's feeling good. Because it's only two and a half months to fishing season.

I do not lust after the fish locators, but I have my own weaknesses. I move about the store like a Boy Scout at a trading post — touching, handling, inspecting.

Make no mistake, I don't need anything. No particular department pulls me. My yearning is aimless. My unsure footsteps follow my drifting eyes.

Fishing reels. Black and beautiful, with their quick triggers and skirted spools and graphite composition — graphite, to save weight. As if drifting a leech all day for walleyes is going to strain my wrist.

My gaze caresses the climbing gear — seat harnesses, reels full of nylon webbing, climbing shoes, nuts, chocks, ascenders. I am not a climber, but I wish I were. The gear is worth the lusting.

Campstoves, candle lanterns, headlamps, "organizer" bags for camp kitchens, genuine Swiss Army knives. I try not to drool on the glass counter.

On. On to the Helly-Tech rain gear and Patagonia lustibles. Tactel and Synchilla and Capilene — miracle fabrics that I must fluff and paw. Fabrics with price tags I must ogle and avoid.

I move up to the front of the shop and start over again. This time I'm trolling for fishing tackle. Little tiny boxes of hooks and jigs and jig paint and split-shot sinkers.

And rods. Oh, the gleaming of them. None of their guides have been smushed sideways by a portly Duluth pack. None of their tips have been foreshortened by the fateful slam of a car door. None of their sleek bodies have been marred by the grit of a canoe floor.

I gently disengage a rod from its padded display slot. I flick it. Six feet of response. Four ounces of sensitivity. Four hours of take-home pay. I put it back.

Spoons and jigs and spinners take me back to the

camping goods again. Oh, no. Nalgene bottles. My most vulnerable area. They are just quart-size, wide-mouth vessels, but they are the BMW of water bottles. I fondle and price one. A mere $3.50. A pittance for a quart of quality. But it goes back on the shelf. I have a box full of them at home.

I am just about to veer toward the maps when I see another acquaintance enter the shop. He seems to have a purpose to his step. He needs a new campstove, he says. A single-burner. "I'm tired of dragging the old two-burner around in the canoe," he says.

We talk stoves. We talk fuel. Then we're talking Basswood Lake and big walleyes and — we both see it coming — The Fishing Opener.

Finally, I break away. I sense it is time. Sure, he wants to look at stoves. Might even buy one. But he will want to wander, too. He will likely do some lusting.

He will want to be alone.

Spring Is Humming

I saw my first mosquito of the year the other day. It was humming around my face. I was sitting with a dog-sledding friend of mine in his cabin near Ely.

At first I didn't even recognize the sound. I thought it was coming from a fly with engine problems. Then I caught the familiar blurred hovering, and reality set in. Next thing I knew, there were two of them.

"They're tame," my friend said. "But don't turn your back on them. They'll bite."

I escaped unsmitten, but I'll have to admit it was good to see those leggy critters again. They were tangible, tactile evidence that a new season was upon us. But then, the whole day had produced signs of the coming spring.

That morning I had hitched a ride on a U.S. Forest Service flight. From 500 feet up we had observed eagles incubating eggs. The big birds have been on eggs since about April 1, said the Forest Service wildlife biologist.

In a marshy retreat near Low Lake, we saw a couple of scruffy moose slurping aquatic vegetation. The biologist said moose rely on aquatic vegetation — roots of water lilies, for instance — for sodium. Whatever the case, it was good to see a moose knee-deep in anything except snow. It looked right.

That afternoon, making the 20-minute walk into my friend's cabin, I had come upon the new season again. It was oozing from between the alder roots and soaking into sphagnum moss. I usually don't spend much time in the woods in April. No fish to catch or camps to be made, it seems. So I miss the cold seeping out of the ground and the first curls on last fall's aspen leaves as they emerge from winter's press of snow.

The woodpeckers were yammering away, and the flickers were flying that crazy, wings-wrapped-all-the-way-around-the-fuselage flight of theirs. I expected to top a rise and see a mama ruffed grouse slow-footing along with a column of peeping young ones in tow. But I didn't.

What I saw, taking flight from a little beaver pond, were a hen and drake mallard, point-blank, all tailfeathers and wingbeats. She lifted off first, hurling raspy indignation over her primary feathers. He followed, quick and powerful, resplendent in blue speculum.

The mallards circled the pond once, gained altitude, and made a pass directly over my head. I stood and watched them come at me, turn black against the sun, then disappear toward a neighboring lake.

That did it. Life was rolling along too well not to take a short nap. I humped up a ridge, found a hunk of granite the glaciers had left and propped my head on my backpack. For a while I tried to let the sun bake my face, but the day was too bright. I threw my arm over my head and let my body sag into the rock.

I awoke to the sound of someone hammering over at my friend's homestead. Then a sled dog yowled. I lay there for luxurious moments, toasted by the sun, lazy with sleep.

When the time seemed right, I got up and continued down the trail to the cabin and my rendezvous with the mosquitoes.

Before the day was out, I had seen a pair of common mergansers preening next to candled ice on Shagawa Lake, a ruffed grouse poking across a lane and three deer flicking their ears at my intrusion.

April. The North Country was waking.

Tobey

His rods are strung. His reels are full. But Tobey Maki won't be going fishing.

For most of his 84 years Tobey has spent opening day of fishing season on the water. But now Tobey is a sick man.

When Minnesota's walleye season opens, Tobey will probably be right where he was one sunny afternoon this week — sitting in his easy chair in the living room of his home in Ely.

His wife of 47 years, Frances, will be in her chair across the room, next to the big piano. Maybe one of Tobey's friends will stop by. They'll talk. The day will pass.

It just won't be the same, that's all.

I spent opening day with Tobey in 1981. We fished from the bridge at Birch Lake Dam on Highway 1 south of Ely. While we talked fishing, Tobey worked on a chaw of Apple Jack and caught himself a limit of walleyes.

"I take 'em back to the old people," he had said then. He was 81. "I got a lot of people on my list."

It was a good day.

Tobey's troubles started last spring. Kidneys, the doctors said. Two months in two hospitals. No fishing all summer. Then, three or four months ago, it was a heart attack. Somewhere along the way Tobey lost 40 pounds.

When I stopped in to see him this week, I hadn't seen him since our opening day together in '81. I'd thought of him often. I'd been to Ely several times. Just hadn't had time to stop by. You know how it is.

I was sorry about that. Sorry that I hadn't made the time.

Now here Tobey was, slumped in his easy chair, bottles of medicine in a basket on the floor at his side. He wore a plaid flannel shirt and a pair of dark gray work pants. In the gap between his pants and his socks, long underwear was visible. He had on a pair of leather slippers. His aluminum walker was behind a chair nearby.

"Hi, Mr. Cook," he said.

He looked tired. Gone was the sparkle in his blue eyes.

We talked for a while about what it's like to be old and sick. About sleepless nights. About being too weak to take a walk. About the $6,000 that Medicare didn't pay.

Frances seemed to say it best. "Getting old is the bunk," she said. "And nobody knows it 'til they get there."

Tobey seemed listless. His arms appeared to rest heavily on the arms of the chair. Occasionally he'd tap his big fingers. Then he'd be still again.

"He's very, very depressed," Frances said. "The doctor

says he's depressed because he can't do what he wants to do."

What Tobey wants to do, of course, is fish. Until last year, he fished almost every day of the summer. He'd drive his old Buick out to the Birch Lake Dam or to the Garden Lake bridge or maybe out to Halfway bridge. He'd dangle a leech in the water, and he'd catch walleyes.

Oh, did he catch walleyes. Frances would keep track. She remembers writing them down each day the last summer Tobey fished.

"I got to 129, and I quit counting," she said.

Gradually, as we talked about fishing, Tobey began to perk up.

We went back to his days as a guide, working out of Burntside Lodge on Burntside Lake, north of Ely. That was when a guide's wages were $5 a day, or $6 a day on overnight trips.

"Guiding. That was my bread and butter," Tobey said. "I guaranteed fish. If you don't catch fish, you don't owe me anything."

He was sitting up straighter now, gesturing with his arms.

In those days, Tobey said, a guide and his party could fly into the canoe country for day trips. Tobey remembers a lot of those short hops from Burntside into Crooked Lake.

Frances, who was a cabin girl at the lodge, remembers him returning each evening.

"We'd hear the plane, and everyone would go down to the dock to see what they caught," she said.

"I'd dump the gunny sack on the dock, and out would come 4-, 5-, 6-, 7-, 8-pound walleyes," Tobey said.

The conversation drifted.

"You know I went with him for seven years and he never asked me to marry him?" Frances said. "I finally had to put my foot down. I said, 'If you don't want to marry me, don't come to pick me up tomorrow night.'"

I asked Tobey what took him so long.

"I wasn't in any hurry," he said. "And them days, there were lots of fish, hey?"

Beside Tobey's chair, taped to the base of a lamp on the table, was a Polaroid picture. He pulled it off the lamp and passed it over. The picture showed Tobey holding a big walleye in front of him.

"That one was over 11 pounds," he said. "I got it at the Garden Lake bridge. Garden Lake bridge is good for big fish if you know where to go."

Big fish. That reminded Tobey of a story. He was fishing at the Birch Lake Dam one day down below the bridge, from shore. He'd hooked a big northern.

"Fifteen, maybe 16 pounds," he said.

He'd been playing the fish for several minutes. A man fishing from the bridge had been watching him.

"He hollered down at me, 'Get him in, or you're gonna lose him.'"

The man kept hollering at Tobey, trying to hurry him up.

Finally, Tobey replied. "I looked up at him and said, 'Why should I hurry now? I've waited 15 years for this fish.'"

Tobey chuckled, still pleased with his comeback. He'd been leaning forward as he told the story, motioning with his arms. The sparkle was back in his eyes.

"You know what the best bait is? The best bait is still the leech. There's nothing like a leech. And a little hook, about a No. 6. And two small split-shot (sinkers)," he said.

The room was silent for a moment as all of us thought about that. I remembered something Tobey had said on that opening day we spent together. "I'll never quit fishing," he had said. "If I have to crawl on my hands and knees, I'll go fishing."

It had sounded good at the time, but it wasn't working out that way.

"Watcha gonna do?" Tobey said. "The doctor tells you you can't drive that car. You gotta listen to the doctor. I don't want no accident. I got more fish to catch."

Lucky Girl

Somewhere there's a little girl. Four years old. Or five, maybe.

She's like a lot of little girls. She likes Care Bears and Smurfs and Sesame Street. She jumps rope and steps in puddles and loves that out-of-control feeling of running down big hills.

Her shins almost always show a couple of bruises. Her elbows are apt to have thin scabs on them. Learning to ride a bike isn't easy.

This little girl is lucky. Next Saturday she's going fishing.

It's The Opener, you know. She's going up north with Mom and Dad and her little brother. He's only two.

They'll be at this cabin. Pretty neat place. Has a lot of pine needles on the ground. And a dock. That's the neatest thing.

She has her own fishing rod and everything. It's white, and not as long as the ones Mom and Dad use. But it's just right for her. The reel is black and silver.

You push a button and the line slips out. Then you turn the handle and it comes back in. Simple.

She usually sits in the middle when they go out in the boat. Dad runs the motor, and Mom sits up front. The little girl takes her lunch box along. It has her sandwich in it. Peanut butter and jelly. Dad says fish like the smell of peanut butter and jelly.

The lunch box usually has some cookies in it, too, and maybe some nacho cheese chips and carrots. Mom and Dad have their own lunch box. Theirs has sandwiches and pop and maybe a couple of beers in it.

Dad brings the bait, which sometimes is minnows and sometimes is leeches. Minnows are fun. They flip and wiggle when you try to catch 'em in the minnow bucket. Leeches are ishy. Usually Mom or Dad puts the leeches on the hook for the little girl.

She can't figure out why a fish would want to eat a leech, or even another fish, for that matter. 'Specially when they could have peanut butter and jelly or part of a carrot. But Dad says leeches and minnows are what work, so that's what they use.

Sometimes it's sort of boring sitting in the boat. Sometimes the fish aren't hungry, even for leeches and minnows. But the little girl passes the time, mostly by asking questions. Questions like how fast fish swim, and what their eyes are made of, and why fishing line has those curls in it, and how high those clouds are, and how long it would take to drink all the water in the lake, and how fish sleep under water and things like that.

Lots of questions. Sometimes Mom and Dad know the answers to the questions. Sometimes they don't.

Sometimes it's not so fun to be in the boat. That's because Dad gets mad at Mom when she gets these things called snags. Her hook gets caught on a rock or something down in the water, and then Dad has to back up the boat, and Mom thinks, no, maybe it's a fish, and Dad gets this mad look on his face. Usually it isn't a fish. Sometimes Mom has to break the line. Dad doesn't say much for a while after that.

Sometimes Dad gets his hook caught on the bottom, too. But he never says anything about it. He just backs the boat up and gets the hook off or breaks his line. Sometimes Mom laughs about that, but not right out loud.

One time the little girl caught a fish. It was a northern. It had lots of teeth. She reeled it in. Dad swooped it up in the net.

She touched it after it was in the boat. It was wet, and it smelled bad. It made her hand smell bad. Dad put the northern on the stringer, and then he put the stringer in the water.

The little girl had Dad check to make sure the northern was still on the stringer. She had him check lots of times. It was still there every time.

Mom caught some walleyes. Dad didn't catch anything. He said it was because he was too busy working the motor and putting leeches on hooks.

It was a real fun day. When they got back to the cabin that day, she called her Grandma and Grandpa to tell them about her fish. They thought it sounded like a pretty big fish.

She might catch a fish like that next Saturday. They're going to the same lake. She's taking her Care Bear with her.

It's The Opener.

She's lucky.

Summer

Supper and Sauna

We had spent the day fooling a bunch of walleyes. Now we were back at my friend's Rainy Lake cabin, facing the day's big decision: Do we take the boat to the resort across the bay for supper, or do we get in the car and take the road around the bay? The vote was unanimous. The boat.

The sun behind the pines looked like a Minnesota postcard. The spray from the boat had a peachy cast to it, and our skin took on that tawny glow usually reserved for catalog models. Even with the 25-horse peppering us along, a T-shirt was all we needed for comfort.

The cheeseburgers were thick, and the french fries still had skin on them. We paid the waitress and waddled back to the dock. The ride back to the cabin was most notable for the bugs that hit our faces, and for the color of the crescent moon that was already setting. It was the same color the boat spray had been on the way over, with maybe a wash of salmon thrown in.

There are places where I would just as soon not hear

the whine of a boat motor, but this night it seemed to belong. It belonged as much as the lights in cabin windows and the buoys that marked the big lake's channel.

We were getting close to the cabin. I waited for my partner at the throttle to ease the motor down to a purr. I waited for the backwash to come rolling up and push us onto the sand beach. Both the sound and the feeling came right on cue. The bow nudged sand.

We fired up the sauna and killed time until it was ready. Then we climbed onto the top bench. My buddy splashed the Lake Superior stones three hits with water, and we waited for the heat to come around.

Oh, yes.

The day's dirt oozed out of micropores and formed tiny bubbles on red skin. The bubbles joined briny rivulets, which became sweaty streams, which flowed to the cedar bench. We dripped and moaned and swabbed our faces.

Three more hits. The heat came around again.

Sometime after all of this, I found myself standing bare in the night, letting the breeze cool me. I was clean now. Is there a cleaner clean than a sauna-and-drip-dry-in-the-breeze clean? The cave people did a lot of this, I suppose, and the Finns have done their part to carry on the tradition.

But those of us who came by saunas late in life don't do nearly enough of it. Why else would it seem so refreshingly unusual to be standing naked in the night air?

I was tempted to go back in the cabin to grab a cold drink, but I resisted. I wanted to do some star time first. I put damp feet in my running shoes, slipped on a pair of wet shorts, and poked down to the dock. There I lay on my back and stared upward.

I don't know my stars well, but nights like that make

me wish I did. If any of the constellations were missing, they must have sent others to take their places. Presiding over all of the individual wonders was the blur of the Milky Way.

Walleyes. Sunset. Sauna. Stars.

I decided to stay there, grounded on the timbers of the dock, the breeze washing over me, until I saw a falling star. It didn't take long. It was yellow and fast. If the sky had been a clock, the falling star started at about noon, and by the time it reached one o'clock, it burned itself out. But that was good enough for me.

I got up and walked along the dock back to shore. The yellow light looked good coming from the cabin window. I went on in and enjoyed the cold drink I'd been waiting for.

Gust

When you're just even with the old cabin on Blueberry Island, you're getting near the spot.

That's when you want to start paying out your 45-pound-test copper line, letting the 2-ounce sinker carry the Rapala to the bottom of Burntside Lake. You have to be on the bottom.

"You gotta drag bottom to catch fish," Gust Helback said. "No snags, no fish."

It was Helback, 83, who was paying out his ancient copper line, 220 feet of it, so his silver jointed Rapala would drag the unforgiving bottom 70 feet below. The Rapala was affixed to a 2-foot leader of 20-pound monofilament line.

The copper line was still rolling off Helback's Penn No. 49 "Deep Sea" level-wind reel. The process seemed more like a telephone crew laying buried cable than a fisherman preparing to troll. Finally, Helback's thumb and forefinger felt the second knot in the copper line — the mark he was looking for.

"That's it," he said.

He engaged the reel's anti-reverse lever, idled his 6-horse Evinrude to a sleepy sputter and got down to fishing.

Helback is something of a cult figure among anglers in Ely. Week after week, throughout the summer, the gentle old man hauls up big lake trout from Burntside's rocky depths.

Inside Burntside Lodge, on the lake's south shore, Helback's weigh-in slips are posted on a bulletin board.

May 23, lake trout, 12 pounds, 6 ounces, Rapala.

May 23, lake trout, 17 pounds, 4 ounces, Rapala.

June 17, lake trout, 14 pounds, 13 ounces, Rapala.

June 17, lake trout, 5 pounds, 10 ounces, Rapala.

June 29, lake trout, 7 pounds, 0 ounces, Rapala.

Last year, Helback took an 18-pounder, a 12-pounder and a 6-pounder on the same evening. All this from a lake many locals call the Dead Sea.

Helback is revered, respected, envied and copied.

"Just about everyone knows who he is," said Mark Heywood, area fisheries supervisor for the Minnesota Department of Natural Resources at Ely. "And he's known for catching lake trout in Burntside. Nobody else can."

"Nobody brings in the lake trout the way Gust brings in lake trout," said Lonnie LaMontagne, co-owner of Burntside Lodge. "He's a legend."

Other anglers have been known to follow Helback to his hotspot to watch him fish. They call him at home to ask him how he does what he does. They ask to go fishing with him.

He isn't secretive.

"I tell the guys how I fish," Helback said. "I don't try to hide it. I'm not long on this earth anyways."

He rarely takes anyone with him. His only partner is a small blue gasoline can filled with lead that he puts in the bow of his 16-foot Alumacraft for ballast. Helback sits on a boat cushion at the stern, manning his trusty Evinrude 6-horse.

"I'm a loner," he said.

It is not so much his personality as it is a practicality. It makes sense for the way he fishes.

Once Helback has his line out far enough that his "RUPP-ala" — his pronunciation — is chipping along Burntside's rock bottom, he tucks his rod handle under his arm and cradles that industrial-sized reel next to his chest. Then he fixes his eyes on the tip of his three-foot steel rod and watches his Rapala bump the reef.

Inevitably, near the end of each pass over the reef, the Rapala will become snagged, as it has on this first southward pass.

"This is how I work it," Helback said, revving the 6-horse and carving a wide circle in the water.

When he had swung around and begun moving north, the Rapala popped free. That's the simplicity of his system. Another angler's 220 feet of line dangling overboard would just complicate those quick direction changes.

"That's why I'm alone," Helback said.

He headed back north toward Blueberry Island again, retrieving all 220 feet of line along the way. It came in over the two brass pulleys, through the rod's single guide and onto the reel.

Helback made the pulleys. He also made the sinkers of lead sheathed in copper. And his landing net. And the box he keeps his large Rapalas in. The steel reel seat of his rod had been cast at Oliver Mine, where he worked long ago.

When he drew even with the old cabin on the island, he dropped the Rapala in the water again, swung the boat back to the south, idled down, felt for the second knot, locked the reel and got to fishing again.

He did this over and over, tracing a giant figure-eight on Burntside's placid surface. So precise was his pattern that he seemed to be in a groove on a slot car track rather than afloat on a lake.

One could possibly troll the reef conservatively — without hanging up Rapalas on rocks. But that would violate Helback's heeding: no snags, no fish.

Over the years Helback has broken so many lips off his Rapalas that he began replacing the lips instead of buying new lures. He made his own replacements for several years, then ordered them from the Normark Co., which markets the lures in America. Lips — a dollar a dozen.

Then he happened onto a Minneapolis man who told him Normark would repair the lures for him. The company did better than that.

"Last year, I sent in 24 of 'em," Helback said. "They sent me 24 new ones."

Helback finished his second pass through the hole. He had felt a fish, but it wouldn't stay hooked. Back north he went. He had been skeptical of his prospects that evening after rounding Indian Island on the way out to his hotspot.

He had seen no herring gulls on a reef near the island. His gulls mean good luck.

Helback made his third pass over the reef. He looked all the part of the gentleman angler in his brown slacks, apricot short-sleeved shirt, maroon-and-gold suspenders, leather boots and camouflage cap.

A miner most of his life, Helback has been retired for

19 years. He lives in a simple home on Sheridan Street, the main street of Ely. He must spend most of his time caring for his wife of 58 years, Lulu, who is bedridden after having suffered a heart attack.

Though many assume Helback fishes often to catch the fish he does, he gets out only about once a week.

Still, he knows he's a lucky man to be fishing at 83.

"You're goddarn right," he said. "I tell ya. I look back at all my fishin' buddies, and they're all gone. I been livin' on borrowed time for a long time."

Another pass. Another snag. No lake trout.

Helback switched to a gold and black straight Rapala, then to a fluorescent orange jointed Rapala. Nothing doing. So he just talked about the good times.

"Sometimes every time I go through, I get a hit," he said. "But I only keep one or two and then go home."

Though his 18-pounder last year was a big, big Burntside lake trout, Helback believes they grow larger.

"Last summer I had a couple big ones on. They straightened out the split rings (on the Rapalas)," Helback said. "There's big fish in here. Years ago, up in the North Arm, there was a fish. It must have died of old age or something. Came floatin' up. They weighed him. He weighed 42 pounds."

The old days are easy for Helback to talk about, simply because there are so many of them. He spoke of skiing as a child to his father's pasture on the North Arm of Burntside to make sure the cattle had enough hay. He talked of fishing before outboard motors. He talked of fishing before fishing reels.

"The first time I was on Burntside, I was seven years old," he said. "They were logging that shore over there."

He pointed to the lake's south shore. He was talking about the year 1910.

Helback took off the orange Rapala and went to a straight silver Rapala. Again, no go. He went to a larger size Rapala — a No. 18 — as big as a well-fed smelt.

Smelt. That's the problem with Burntside Lake's fishing these days, he contends.

"They ruined this lake with smelt," Helback said. "I'm looking for small fish and get nothing but big ones. Up to about six pounds, that's the best eating."

The DNR's Heywood confirmed Helback's assessment. Smelt were introduced in the lake in the early 1970s, apparently by anglers who used the dead fish as bait. The sperm and eggs from leftover bait pails evidently spawned a population of the baitfish in Burntside.

Clear, cool and 140 feet deep, Burntside was just what the smelt were looking for. The lake trout and walleyes both feed heavily on smelt, Heywood said. Stuffed on smelt, the fish rarely take a second look at an angler's offering.

"They're not going to eat a nightcrawler or a leech or a dinky minnow," Heywood said. "The catch rate is about half (the statewide average), but the weight is double. Really, we've developed a new trophy lake."

Or, as Helback puts it: "It's mostly them goddang big ones."

The catch rate on lake trout is about one per 20 hours of fishing. Heywood said Helback's rate must be significantly better. But, on this night with no gulls on the reef, even Helback wasn't able to take a fish. He was disappointed but not disgusted.

"That's all it is. Ninety percent luck," he said. "And five percent know-how."

He never said what the other five percent was. Maybe that's what drives all those other anglers crazy.

"It's almost like witching," Heywood said. "I don't know how witching works, and I don't know how Gust Helback's fishing works.

"But he is good."

Loomis Lips

You've got your glamour fish of the North — your walleye, your northern, your smallmouth bass.

And then you've got your fish with the image problem — your sucker.

The sucker, like the rainbow trout, is an excellent swimmer. It has been seen jumping eight or nine feet at swift rapids.

Nutritionally, it ranks high because it's low in fat and has only 27 calories an ounce.

The noble sucker may be able to leap tall buildings in a single bound and may taste like pheasant under glass, but people aren't going to break down freezer cases at the store to get at it. For two reasons.

First, it is ugly. Uhhhhhhh-gly. If you've never been privileged to see one close up, it has something like a downspout where its mouth is supposed to be.

I don't care how the sun glints off its scales when it vaults upstream. It still looks like a cross between a vacuum-cleaner attachment and a carp. You're never

going to see the sucker on art prints at the Trout Un-
limited banquet.

Second, it needs a new name. Too many bad con-
notations for the word "sucker." There's one born every
minute.

Even if respectable folks start trying to enhance the
sucker's reputation, it's going to be tough. For instance . . .

"Hey, John," the guy next to you at the office says. "Bev
and I are having some suckers for dinner tonight. Can
you and Jean come?"

No way you and Jean would walk into that one.

I think there is hope, however. Obviously, we can't
change the sucker's appearance. But we can adapt.
When life gives you lemons, make lemonade.

First, we'll rename the species. From now on this
delectable fish shall be known as — are you ready for
this? — the loomis.

Now, there's a handle, huh?

Look it up in the dictionary. It isn't there. That's
what we want, a good clean slate. No negative connota-
tions to fight.

Try it out:

"Hey, catchin' any loomis lately?"

Or, "Now, that's a nice stringer of loomis!"

And imagine the bait and tackle spinoffs:

"The Little Loomis Slayer!" (Doesn't that slide off your
tongue nice?)

Or, "Hey, you got any o' them loomis leeches?"

But that's just half the battle. We've got to change
that homely mouth from a debit into a credit. And we
can do it, loomis lovers. Because we're gonna market
that snout to snooty folks back east as a delicacy.

That's right: loomis lips.

Can you imagine a heaping plateful of sauteed

loomis lips served up alongside some broccoli lyonnaise? Lordy, it makes your mouth water just thinking about it.

They aren't going to be cheap, understand. Couple reasons for that. One is that removing loomis lips is a very touchy operation. Takes some time. And a sharp knife. Plus, it's going to take a lot of handiwork to get a meal's worth of those circular little things accumulated.

So, by the time they get to the menu in fancy script lettering, they're going to run you about $11.50, including choice of soup or juice, salad and rolls. Which is just fine with those Easterners. The higher the price, the better. You put loomis lips on the menu at $2.75 and those country-club types would never see 'em.

The best thing is, of course, that once we get all those ugly lips shipped out of the Midwest, we're going to have some decent-looking, good-tasting fish left here for us to eat.

Don't laugh. This'll work. Just give it some time.

Remember, it used to be sturgeon eggs were just sturgeon eggs. Until somebody decided they should be caviar.

Somewhere Else

The map lies there, spread across a desk top that is begging for attention.

But the man behind the desk has forgotten all about the clutter beneath the map. He is somewhere else and has been for some time now.

This happens to him often. He realizes that. It happens almost every time he digs out a map of the back country.

He had gotten the map out to locate a hiking trail. He had found it, all right. But that was quite a while ago.

Now he is looking at all that country spread across his desk. All the lakes and rivers and portages. All that country he hasn't covered yet.

Every time he gets to looking at a map like that, he gets to thinking. Is he getting out in the woods enough? Is this urban existence getting too good a hold on him? How is he ever going to see all that country before he dies?

He is 33 years old. He's covered a lot of country in

his time. But he can't help it. He finds himself multiplying by two and getting 66. He can count on one hand the number of 66-year-olds he's seen in the woods.

He'd like to think he'll be out there at 66, that the next 33 years will be as productive as the past 33. But he's not so sure things will work out that way. And he sees all those places on the map he can't yet match with images from his memory: Loon Falls, Beatty Portage, Devil's Cascade. He would like to know what those places look like.

He gets great satisfaction from looking at maps of country where he's been. He follows routes with his eyes that he has traveled with paddle and pack. It feels good, not just to be able to say he's been there, but simply to know what's out there.

Somehow, he enjoys a better sense of who he is from knowing where he is.

His eyes dart from feature to feature: Swanson's Bay, Dawson Portage, Harrison Narrows.

He wonders who Swanson and Dawson and Harrison were. He bets they covered some ground in their day. He wouldn't have minded being around in that time, exploring country that still needed exploring.

He might have missed the bug dope and the aluminum canoes and the lightweight food. But he could have gotten along just fine without the wilderness travel permits and the 40-member church groups.

He scans the map again. He wonders if Swanson and Dawson and Harrison ever hunkered over a map, dreaming of places they'd like to see.

Probably.

He wonders if Swanson and Dawson and Harrison saw all the country they wanted to in their time.

Probably not.

Fall

Last Leaf

The tree stood tall and straight, just off the road.

The road was the Sawbill Trail, a gravel artery that noses into the woods north of Tofte, Minnesota. The tree was an aspen.

The aspen wasn't any different from thousands of others that make the drive up the Sawbill so pleasant. But its few remaining leaves, gold and dry, were shaking in the northwest wind. Every now and then a few would part from their branches and flutter to earth.

That's what I was looking for. I had come to watch one leaf fall. I had found my tree.

Don't get me wrong. I had already seen plenty of leaves fall. I spent one technicolor day chasing grouse when the wind was blowing. That was a couple of weeks earlier. It had rained yellow.

I had walked flaming maple corridors and seen the North Shore's mini-mountains in their spawning colors.

But that was grand and glorious. Now I wanted something small and simple. I wanted to see the season's lowest common denominator. I didn't want a majestic morning. I wanted a magic moment.

I watched where the wind was taking the big aspen's leaves. I took up a position in a small clearing nearby. I waited for the tree to send me a leaf.

I was sitting amid a thousand — maybe a million — aspen and birch leaves that had already dropped. They were brown and gold and yellow and splotched and wet and mottled and crisp and pungent. They were history.

They had fallen to help make more soil, the stuff that's so precious around here. It's been 10,000 years since the last Ice Age. What do we have, a foot or so of humus? A thousand years to the inch? We need all the leaves we can get.

This, I suppose, is why we tend to think of leaves in such sweeping terms. Still, each leaf must decide, in whatever way leaves decide, exactly when it is time to fall. One moment the leaf is quivering there, hanging on by whatever juices allow it to cling. The next moment it is airborne — drifting, spinning, falling to its next appointed purpose on Earth.

I was thinking about those things when another good gust came out of the northwest. The aspen's branches waved. A few leaves said good-bye. None of them, however, floated to the spot where I sat. I hadn't found my leaf yet.

The ground's wetness was beginning to seep through the bottom of my jeans. I waited.

A couple of gusts later, it happened. One leaf was whisked out of the tree and came sailing my way. It made a free-fall of five, six, seven seconds. It didn't spin or twirl, just made partial rotations and flotations. It seemed a slow, lazy flight at the beginning, but as it came closer, I realized it was falling fast.

The leaf drifted just over my head and behind me, but it never reached the ground. Its slender stem wedged between two sapling branches that rubbed together, and the leaf hung there a foot off the ground. It was still catching some breeze, and I thought it might complete its journey in a moment. But it didn't.

Its stem was pale yellow, pinky peach at its base. The leaf itself was a parched yellow, flecked with brown. It was catching the late afternoon sun, and it glowed with backlight.

I wondered about the leaf's future. Would it be consumed by some late-hatching insect and never reach the ground? Would it be blown or rained or snowed to the ground, begin its sweet rotting process and become a condominium for insects in March? Would it be ironed by the weight of winter's snow, heave a silent sigh next April, bake in the May sun and gather dust from northbound pickups come fishing season?

I thought about those prospects as I studied the leaf. I thought if I sat there long enough, it might fall and answer at least one of my questions. It never did.

Brule Guide

It was going to be chilly. We could see our breath at supper. We knew it would be a cold paddle down the river that night.

There would be just the two of us: my friend the Brule River guide and myself. Two of us and a fly rod and several layers of clothing. Our pretense was to fish for the Brule's brown trout, but both of us knew the fish were just a good excuse to be someplace we loved to be.

Wisconsin's Brule River is a wonderful place to find yourself at sunrise. It is a good place to be at midday, when the sun comes piercing through the white pines. But until you have paddled and fished the Brule at night — preferably in September — you have yet to take in all the Brule has to offer.

At the Stone's Bridge landing we had peeled our city clothes and gotten into river gear. An hour later, just about the time the whippoorwills began calling, we were preparing supper. In the best tradition of river guides, we had brought steak, potatoes and onions. One of us had shown up with some pineapple juice, too, but when the other broke out a small bottle of wine, the juice went unopened. Dinner tasted good, but the fire felt better.

Darkness had swallowed the forest when we packed and got back in the canoe. The guide tied a small cork popper called a Hank's Creation on the fly line. I fished. He paddled. The river slipped beneath us.

Now it was all feel and smell and listen. Night air chilled our nostrils. Our hands told us all we needed to know about the fly line and the paddle. When a deer moved across the river ahead of us, our ears told us first.

Sight is a subtle sense when you're paddling the Brule at night. You know you're drifting downstream when you see stars sliding behind a cedar bough. But you're more apt to have already sensed it by the way the river was pushing on your canoe paddle.

We talked a little. We talked about our kids and brown trout and how cool the water was. We talked about the stars. We talked about how tired we'd be at the office the next day.

I caught a six-inch brown trout. We tossed it back to the river. Not much farther along, we traded places in the canoe so the guide could fish. The moon was dropping now, and our hands were cool most of the time. We heard a few fish rolling, but not many.

Then we heard one that sounded thick and heavy. Had we been fishing in the daylight, we might have seen the fish, or at least part of it. It might not have been as large as it sounded. But being spared visual confirmation, we were free to imagine the trout as large as we wished.

My friend worked the sound with his Hank's Creation, but the fish was having none of it. We moved on. The guide caught a 14-inch brown. Like the smaller one, it was returned to the river.

After a time we put the rod away and just paddled. We ran a couple of small riffles, then the chute that guides call "The Falls."

If you are interested in checking the state of your heart, you will want to run some rapids at night. You would be wise to do it with one who knows the river as well as my friend the guide does. It is one thing to miss a rock you can see. It is quite another to avoid one you can only hear as it parts the river's current.

In the bow my partner moved the canoe left or right with quick pulls on his paddle. In the stern I copied his moves. When the moon was directly behind us, I could see the moonshadows of my paddle strokes on my partner's back. Through several sets of riffles, we never touched a rock.

We listened to four deer flee from Big Lake, a widening in the Brule. We passed a canoe. Presumably, it had a couple of anglers in it. Nobody spoke.

It was after 11:00 p.m. when we reached the guide's cabin dock. Neither of us had spoken for the last 15 minutes on the river. I'm not sure why.

It had seemed enough just to have that moist air washing past our faces, just to feel the canoe surging forward with our synchronized strokes, just to be out there under all those stars.

I remember feeling very sleepy. And very alive.

Hawk Ridge

It couldn't be a better day up here.

I am standing at the lip of a sheer hillside in east Duluth, six hundred feet above Lake Superior.

The day is clear and unSeptemberly warm. The trees, of which I can see about a million, are showing their first blush of color. In the great blue beyond, anglers' boats crawl about on the water like aquatic ants.

It would be a good day just for those reasons. But it is even better than that: The hawks are flying.

I have come to Hawk Ridge, as I do too few times each September, to see if the hawks are moving. Hawk Ridge is simply an extension of the range of hills that parallel the North Shore of Lake Superior. But here, at the western tip of the greatest lake, passes one of the largest concentrations of hawks in America each fall. Southbound hawks, instinctively avoiding the expanse of Lake Superior, are drawn to the updrafts created around the tip of the lake — right over this ridge.

I check in with Mark Stensaas, the chief counter for

the Hawk Ridge Nature Reserve. If you go to Hawk Ridge, you will have no trouble spotting Stensaas, a 24-year-old naturalist. He is the one with the rowdy brown beard and the short ponytail. If it is sunny, he'll likely be wearing his llama-wool hat. It's a broad-brimmed lid that makes him look as if he's sitting under a porch roof.

It is Stensaas who quantifies this passage of hawks. Armed with high-powered binoculars and a borrowed 20-power spotting scope, he verifies the eagles and ospreys and sharpshins and kestrels that come buzzing this knoll. A National Geographic Society *Birds of North America* field guide lies at his feet. He rarely has to use it.

Stensaas operates from a folding chair near his car. On his lap lie a clipboard and gridded sheets of paper titled "Hawk Migration Data Sheets." The jottings he scratches on the paper in black ink look like something a chickadee with muddy feet might make.

On the ground near Stensaas are his running shoes with socks rolled neatly inside, a partially empty jar of Ragu Mini Lasagna and a fork.

For years Molly Evans did the bird counting here. It is a good job, despite the low pay, for one who loves to watch birds. But even at that, it can get old. Finally, Evans gave up the job. But not the watching. Today she is standing right beside Stensaas, leaning on his car, scanning the sky with her binoculars.

It isn't that she's worried about Stensaas' competence.

"I like it here," she says.

"Sharpshin," Stensaas says.

He says things like that often, to no one in particular, to anyone within earshot. Then he makes another chickadee scratch on the data sheet.

Today he has made more than five hundred marks in

the sharpshin row on his paper. The birds just keep coming. One low over the hill. Another down the ridge, against the trees where it's hard to pick them up. One comes swooping in to make a pass at the owl decoy just below the ridge.

Stensaas finishes another hour's counting period and marks the sharpshin total in a square: 49. The previous hour's tallies working back toward 8:00 a.m. are 55, 147, 192, 67, 15 and 2. These are just the sharpshins, small hawks with long tails and rounded wings.

Today Stensaas has also seen two turkey vultures, one goshawk, a few kestrels and some broadwing hawks.

"It's a sharpshin day. That's for sure," Stensaas says.

Five hundred sharpshins is a lot, but nothing like the fifteen hundred that moved through on this same day in 1978. But if you want to talk volume, you must talk about broadwings. On that same day — September 15, 1978 — counters at Hawk Ridge tallied almost thirty-two thousand broadwings. It was the most hawks of one species ever recorded in a single day of hawk-watching at the Ridge.

"Here comes an osprey, I think," Stensaas says, glassing the hillside with his ten-powers.

Without binoculars, I can't see the osprey. Stensaas tracks it down the shore. He also sees sharpshins I never see.

"You could sit here all day, and without binoculars, you'd miss fifty percent of them," Stensaas says. "There were eleven thousand hawks over the weekend, and you'd have missed seventy-five percent of them. Everything was so high."

The ones nobody misses are the ones that come by at eye level. Today they are sharpshins. Maybe they have made a pass at the dummy owl. Now they go flapping by, close enough so you can see the bars on their tails and the light spots on their faces. You can see the way they hold their feet. You can watch the way they make the fine adjustments in tailfeathers or wings that keep them aloft and on track.

Here comes one now. He dives at the owl, realizes he has been duped and climbs again. He is oblivious to the humans who cling to this ridge not thirty feet away. He coasts, flaps twice, catches an updraft and rises three feet without a wingbeat.

It is impossible to stand here and not be infected with the spirit of flight. You can watch ten, twenty, fifty — even five hundred hawks — and never get tired of it. You cannot help but wish you could try it yourself, even for a minute or two.

You want so much to know what it would feel like to catch one of those updrafts, to rise, to let the wind work through your primary feathers, to part the air with the little tufts atop your head, to know you had come from Ontario that morning or Manitoba the day before, that you had flapped and glided every bit of the way under your own power.

You cannot help wondering, standing there, watching the hawk passage, just how these birds know that now is the time and this is the way. You wonder how so many of them at one time have felt the strange stirrings from a sense we can only imagine and have decided to move south. You wonder what they must think, especially the young ones, upon encountering this great blue detour called Lake Superior.

You wonder about all of those things, watching Stensaas count hawks on a sharpshin day at Hawk Ridge.

Country Welcome

The little pickup cruised into the farmyard and coasted to a stop. The three of us up front unfolded ourselves and piled out. For a moment we stood there in the dark, listening to the quiet and smelling the pungence of the farm.

The silence was total, and the farm smelled of wet hay. It is a smell that, if you were raised in farm country, comes wrapping itself around you with memories of big midday meals, kittens at the back door and the clank of hog feeders out by the barn.

This Minnesota farm snug by the South Dakota line belongs to Goodman and Marge Larson, and it was Goodman — they call him "Goodie" — who came stepping out the back door to welcome us. The three of us who had been sardined in the pickup were Gary Larson, who is Goodie and Marge's son, Steve Harrington, and me.

We had come to the Larson farm to hunt pheasants, but as sometimes happens on hunting trips, good things begin to occur before you ever set foot in the field or marsh. That is what invariably happens at Marge and Goodie's.

For starters Goodie came out of the house talking about possible hunting plans for the next morning. At 72 he still chases pheasants with the enthusiasm of a 15-year-old. We hauled in shotguns and packsacks while Goodie recounted his hunts from the previous few days. The mood was set.

Inside, the farmhouse glowed with warmth. There are magazines devoted to decorating country places until they look like the Larson home, but theirs comes by it naturally. It's been in the family since 1917.

Its wooden floors are dressed up only by throw rugs. The kitchen is simple, with the oil stove prominent at the north end. The big table seems to invite you to sit down for a cup of coffee.

Just off the kitchen is the bathroom, and that's where you find out you really belong at the Larsons'. Marge had a towel and a washcloth hanging up for each of us. Next to each towel was a piece of masking tape with each of our names on it. Marge's purpose was organization; the effect was that you felt you'd come home.

On a coffee table in the living room was Goodie's hunting journal. Each of his recent hunts was described for posterity in blue-ink handwriting. In vases around the room stood dried wildflowers and native prairie grasses that Goodie had brought back from walks. Prairie plants with bird nests entwined in the branches were stapled to the walls upstairs. More of Goodie's gatherings.

Just outside the kitchen window, though you can't see them at night, were the bird feeders. In the coming days, they would offer sunflower seeds and suet to white-breasted nuthatches, tree sparrows, downy woodpeckers and chickadees. Goodie and Marge can point out each species. They know their birds as well as they know their prairie grasses.

The point is, when you come to the Larson farm to hunt pheasants, you find you are moving in with people you'd like to have not only as friends and hunting companions, but as grandparents or biology professors.

Marge was gathering us around the table now. It was time to have some of her carrot cake in honor of Goodie's recent birthday. She served the cake. Someone poured coffee. We ate.

Sometime after the catching-up conversation tapered off, I walked out the back porch, past the hunting coats and rubber boots, down the back steps and out onto the grassy spot under the yard light. I did it to smell the hay again, to feel the mellow dampness of this November night and to take a deep whiff of country air.

I stood there for a couple of minutes, not thinking so much as feeling, when I heard the porch door open again. It was Harrington, coming out to let his Lab run one more time. He walked over to where I was standing. We didn't say much, but I imagine he was feeling the same things I was. About how good it was to be breathing that air. About how much Marge and Goodie make you feel like part of the family. About hunting pheasants in the morning.

We thought about those things for a minute. Then Harrington called his dog, and we headed for the light at the back door.

Tootsie Roll Midgees

The deer hunter has been sitting on the moss-covered log for almost an hour now, and he's cold. His toes are cold. His fingers are cold. The small of his back, still damp with sweat from his quarter-mile trek to the deer stand, is cold, too.

Making matters worse, the sun refuses to rise from behind the ridge at the hunter's back. The sun is teasing him, lighting up the tips of the popple branches he faces. The hunter is jealous of the branches basking in the warm light of the sun.

The amber glow inches slowly, slowly down the branches. It will be hours before it descends the trunks, creeps across the forest floor and reaches the hunter in the lee of the ridge.

From somewhere off in the trees comes a muted croak. It sounds like a raven gargling. A weird image appears in the hunter's mind: a raven perched on its bathroom sink, peering into its medicine chest mirror, gargling.

Such are the thoughts that invade the mind of a deer hunter.

He reaches slowly into the pocket of his blaze orange coat and feels around, sorting through .30-30 cartridges, broken bits of twigs and a flashlight until he finds what he's after. A Tootsie Roll Midgee. Tootsie Roll Midgees make good deer-hunting candy. Their waxy wrappers come off with scarcely a sound. No matter how cold the weather, the candy softens into chewy sweetness when warmed between cheek and gums.

The hunter has more Tootsie Roll Midgees with him than he has .30-30 cartridges. He knows which he is more apt to need.

Sitting on a deer stand is hard work. It wouldn't appear hard to the casual passer-by. But the casual passer-by can't see the cold toes and fingers, or feel the dull ache where the hunter's posterior and the moss-covered log meet. The moss cushions the hunter, but at a price. It was frosty when the hunter arrived this morning, and his body heat has slowly thawed the ice crystals. Now he can feel the dampness through his wool pants.

But the hardest work of sitting on a deer stand is mental. Sitting on a log without speaking, without squirming, remaining vigilant — or at least awake — is difficult for this hunter.

He simply watches and thinks. He watches the sunlight drip down the branches. Watches the sky grow from black to blue-black to blue. Watches the frost on fallen aspen leaves become water again.

He thinks about ravens gargling, about whether a deer is watching him at this very moment, about how much longer he can sit there without getting up to relieve himself. He thinks about his wife, about his job, about where he'll be in five years. He thinks about

whether his rifle will shoot straight if given the opportunity, about whether he has chosen the best location,
about what he'll do if a deer approaches from behind
instead of in front.

He thinks about having another Tootsie Roll Midgee.

How many thoughts can a deer hunter think in a day
on a deer stand? A thousand? Fifty thousand? A million?

Rifle shots pierce the hush. Distant rifle shots. Two,
three, four of them in rapid succession. The hunter
remembers an old Indian guide's saying: "One shot —
deer. Two shot — deer maybe. Three shot — no deer."

The hunter shifts his weight, trying to find some
moss that hasn't been compressed yet. No luck.

He rotates his head slowly to see where the sun is. He
can't believe it. It is only two fingers above the ridge.
When the sun is near the horizon, deer hunters always
mark time in fingers. Each finger thickness on an ex-
tended arm represents 15 minutes. One hour to a hand.

He is rotating his head slowly back to straight ahead
when he notices on a deadfall nearby a shape that looks
like a cat's face. Then he sees the rest of the body. It is a
pine marten, looking straight at him. It freezes, stares,
then tiptoes casually off the deadfall and across the
forest floor. The hunter has seen only one marten
before in his life.

That is one of the fringe benefits of deer hunting,
seeing denizens of the forest going about their daily
business. But the hunter would rather see a deer.

A couple of Tootsie Rolls later, the sun is two hands
high. From above comes the whisper of wingbeats. It is
a raven, headed for a highway nearby, perhaps hoping
it will come upon a hare that has been killed by a car in
the night. The hunter smiles. He can't help but wonder
if the raven gargled this morning. If the hunter made

meals of road-killed rabbits, he thinks, he sure would want to gargle in the morning.

Chickadees chatter and cling precariously to small branches as they feed. A gray jay swoops by, two feathers missing from one of its wings. A woodpecker comes to work on a birch just a few feet from the hunter, but other trees prevent him from seeing the bird.

The forest is alive with everything except deer.

The hunter studies his rifle for a while, then his boot-laces and, finally, the inside of his eyelids. He lets the sleep come, doesn't fight it. It feels good, dropping off.

He is awakened by the sound of something walking through the woods. He moves his thumb to the hammer of his lever-action Marlin. The footsteps are getting nearer, louder. But they don't sound as if they belong to a whitetail. Not unless this whitetail is walking on its hind legs and wearing heavy pac boots.

After several minutes the hunter glimpses a red coat and orange pants. The other hunter emerges into the clearing. The two wave to each other, silently, and the walking hunter disappears into the forest.

The hunter is alone again. He would like nothing more than to get up and go for a walk, to stretch his legs, to see something other than the scene before him, which he has memorized.

But he sits. The remainder of his day will be punctuated by a peanut butter and jelly sandwich, an apple and some milk. In his pockets, the Tootsie Roll wrappings soon will outnumber the Tootsie Rolls.

The sun will drop low into the southwest. Two hands. One hand. Three fingers. Two. One.

The hunter will get up off his log and walk out of the forest.

Deer hunting is hard work.

Hunting Coat

The night was crisp, and the moon looked good through the bare branches of a maple tree.

The dog and I were making our usual late-night trot around the block, so as to secure the territory until morning. I left that mostly to Dave, the shaggy setter-Lab who had me tethered to the other end of his rope leash.

I was wearing my hunting coat, as I often do on these nightly jaunts. Its heavy cotton duck felt good, and the coat had a convenient pocket for my non-leash hand. I like to think that's why I was wearing the coat.

But I know that at least part of the reason I wear that jacket is that I don't get to wear it near enough in the places it's meant to be worn. Places like grassy swales and cattail lowlands and alder tangles.

I don't get to wear it near enough when its pockets are heavy with shotgun shells and full of little broken twigs and weed seeds. I will never get enough hours in that jacket with a rooster pheasant's tailfeathers poking out of the game bag.

And so, when it's 10:00 p.m. and the dog is standing with his nose at the crack of the door, I slip into the coat, and we walk.

I got to thinking about all of this as the dog and I were nearing the apogee of our nightly circuit, down on the side street where the maple stood naked against the moon and stars. I got to thinking about all the hunting gear I've accumulated over the course of birthdays and Christmases the past few years.

I've gotten the vest I'd looked at autumn after autumn. I've gotten the shooting gloves and the Goretex parka and the buffalo-plaid wool shirt and the camouflage field bag. And, of course, the coat.

The dog stopped to sniff some grass. He seemed to detect that another dog had intruded on his domain since our walk the night before. He raised his leg and reclaimed the turf.

I was thinking about all of this gear I'd accumulated and how little time I seem to spend in it. A couple of times in the last week I'd been talking to friends who also were lamenting the way October was sneaking away from us and how little they'd been afield. It didn't matter that one of them had already spent nine days big-game hunting and that the other would be leaving in a few days for a 12-day South Dakota pheasant hunt. It still seems as if we spend too many days walking past the pegs in the hall where those vests and coats hang.

All too often, these days, we have more money to spend on decoys and duck calls than we have time to use them.

I remember when I was a kid and the dog in front of me was an orange and white pointer named Chico. He wasn't on a leash, and he didn't much care what other dogs were in his territory as long as there were plenty of quail and pheasants around.

But I wasn't thinking so much about Chico as I was the clothes I wore then. Bluejeans and cotton long-johns. A flannel shirt and a hooded sweatshirt. Maybe a seven-dollar vest from Sears. Last summer's baseball cap. A pair of leather boots that had spent most of the summer walking on hay bales in barns. The sweatshirt was full of little frayed holes across the back from too many quick passages under barbed wire fences. The boots usually didn't have enough laces to go all the way to the top.

But we hunted. Weekends it was with Dad and the old Falcon station wagon on Walt Fund's road south of town. After school it was often a tromp from home out to Larry Bailey's land next to the golf course. And there was always a covey on the golf course in the woods be-tween the Number Four and Number Five fairways.

I wish I had a nickel for every burr and every seed I plucked out of that old blue sweatshirt. I wish I had a penny for every scratch I put into the back of my left hand walking through thickets trying to keep my gun up.

I never remember having more than one box of shells at a time. It was always a big day when Dad would slip me three dollars and send me into Davis Hardware for another box of No. 7 1/2's.

Those memories had carried me down to the corner, under the street light, where Dave was anointing the light pole. A small puff of steam rose into the night air. I stood and waited while Dave scuffed grass toward the pole, just for good measure.

What I'm getting at, I guess, is that the hunts were never any sweeter than they were in sweatshirts and jeans. It's nice to have the coat and the shooting gloves and the fancy boots now, but somehow they haven't improved my shooting or made the dried weeds any more intoxicating on an October morning.

The afternoon hunts we stole at Larry Bailey's when we were counting our shells were every bit as rewarding as the trips I now make to South Dakota with a hundred dollars and a VISA card in my wallet. Seems there were plenty of the former hunts, and there aren't near enough of the latter.

Dave and I turned and headed for home. Someone was burning wood, and the smoke smelled good. I unclipped the leash and let Dave in the back door.

And hung my hunting coat on the hook in the hallway.

Winter

Cool Camping

It was seven below zero. The wind was whistling out of the northwest at about 15 miles an hour. Seemed like a good night to sleep outside.

I grabbed my sleeping bag and a couple of foam pads, slipped into my parka and a pair of Polarguard booties, kissed my sweetie good night — and headed out.

The snowhouse was waiting, right where I'd left it. It was about 15 feet from the back porch, and about midway between the crabapple tree and the blue spruce.

It was a simple home. A one-bedroom model with the crawl-through entrance on the uphill side. I had built the snowhouse over the weekend after 19 inches of snow had fallen.

I had started shoveling in large, concentric circles, piling the snow to the inside. After about four revolutions, I had a heap of snow about five feet high and ten feet in diameter.

The next step, I knew, was to poke foot-long sticks into the heap of snow. That way, when you're under all the snow, hollowing out your home's interior, you know where you are. You hit a stick, you don't dig any farther. When you've hit all the sticks, you have a nice home with foot-thick walls.

But I'd done this mostly in the woods before, where sticks are plentiful. I wasn't so keen on pruning my crabapple tree, but I broke off four or five branches anyway and stuck them into my pile at strategic points.

After two or three hours I had gone back out with a Melmac plate and had begun carving out my house. It turned out a little smaller than I thought it might be — sort of an intimate one-bedroom home. But that was all right. I didn't figure I'd have much company when it came time to sleep there.

I didn't realize how much the roof of the dome home had sagged until I went shuffling out there with my booties and bag. I'd never had a snowhouse sag like that before. I didn't figure it would be covered by my homeowner's policy, so I risked poking through the roof and carved another few inches off the ceiling. No problem.

The house still wasn't large enough to sit up in, but I could prop myself up on one elbow to light the candles. Ahhh, that was nice. You haven't experienced the definition of the word "glow" until you've been in a snowhouse lit by candles.

The white walls take on a warm, yellow hue that seems to be more of a presence than simply a light. But it isn't enough of a presence to keep your fingertips from freezing.

I slithered out of my jeans and into the sleeping bag, which is a lot more difficult than it sounds. Every time my head or an elbow or a knee would brush against the ceiling, a fine spray of snow crystals would come to rest on my face or down my neck or in my bag.

I wriggled out of my parka and rolled it loosely to form a pillow. Then I blew out the candles, cinched down my sleeping bag hood and listened to the quiet.

I'm not sure what it's like to be in a tomb. I haven't talked with anyone who's been there. But I think it must be a lot like lying in a snowhouse with a sagging roof.

As I lay in my bag, looking up, the roof was no more than five inches from my face. I could see it reflecting the moonlight that was beaming on the snow in the tunnel entrance.

I could hear no sounds from the outside world. No cars in the streets. No hum of the city. No neighborhood dogs barking.

Remember that feeling you got in grade school when the nurse put you in the booth for the hearing test? That's like the hush of a snowhouse.

It was some time before I fell asleep. I remember my nose feeling cold four or five times. I remember the moisture that had begun to gather around the grapefruit-sized opening in my sleeping bag hood.

Sometime during the night, as the moon made its trip across the city, my body heat escaping from the Quallofil sleeping bag must have warmed the house. My nose was never cold again. I rolled over once or twice, scraping snow from the ceiling with my shoulders each time.

Finally, I woke up and wasn't tired. The moonlight seemed especially bright in the tunnel. I retrieved an arm from the depths of the bag, put my face to my watch and looked at the numbers:

6:54 a.m. Tuesday the 3rd of December.

Yep, that was the day I was supposed to get up. The moonlight that seemed so bright was daylight.

I snaked out of the bag and out of the snowhouse. I

stood up and saw my shadow, which I think meant six more months of winter. I glanced at the thermometer: 10 below zero. I shuffled inside and kissed my sweetie good morning.

Woodstove

I lifted the lid off the woodstove and poked at the coals of hard maple inside. They shot sparks the way they always do, and the warmth came billowing up at my face.

I stood there for a moment, stirring the coals, watching the orange glow. I like loading the woodstove. I like the mild scent of woodsmoke that comes wafting up from the big iron box.

The wood — maple and birch — is piled on skids just across from the stove in our basement. Sometimes the wood is stacked neatly, but more often it is in the same jumbled heap that it landed in when it was tossed in the window.

I would like to say that wood is the only source of heat in our home. Not that I have any back-to-the-land ideals, but because I'd like to think my life was simple enough to heat that way. It isn't. Our home is modest, but too big for one basement woodstove. And our come-and-go habits don't lend themselves to wood heat.

So the old oil furnace kicks in and hums away nearby, not as often as it would if we didn't have the woodstove, but several times a day and often at night.

I don't burn wood to save money. I burn wood because for about the same money as I'd spend on oil alone I can make the house much more comfortable.

I surely don't burn wood because I enjoy handling it. I used to have wood delivered in eight-foot lengths. Then I'd cut it and split it. Then one year, for a few dollars more, I had it delivered cut. That was better. Now I have it delivered cut and split. That's better yet, but I'm thinking about having it stacked next year.

They say wood warms you twice — once in the cutting and once in the burning. Anyone who has burned wood knows that isn't true. It warms you about six times, even if you don't cut your own.

It warms you when toss it to the person who's stacking it, and it warms him when he's stacking it. Then it warms you some winter night when you take it off the stack and pull it on your sled to the house. It warms you again when you take it off the sled and toss it in the basement. Some of it warms you again when you pick it up off the basement floor by the dog's bed and put it back on the skid pile. And, finally, it warms you when you take it off the skid and put it in the stove — even if you're already warm.

If you want to take it one step further, it warms you indirectly when you sweep all the dried leaves and bits of bark off the basement floor when you're finished.

But I still like burning the stuff.

Have you ever lain on the livingroom carpet in that sweet spot right over the stove? Have you felt that deep, slow heat melt into your body and soothe your bones?

Have you ever stood over a well-stoked woodstove in

damp ski clothes? Have you ever warmed red and aching hands by holding them just out of sear range over the stove top?

And have you ever found a better way to slow-dry cross-country ski gloves, polypropylene long johns, wool pants, felt boot liners, tent ground cloths, pile caps, fleece jackets and your daughter's potty training accidents?

There's something about that heat. It's gentle and patient. It doesn't come hurrying out of some metal grate in your livingroom wall. It radiates out and up, seeping through the livingroom floor, filling the room, wrapping itself around you, penetrating, lasting.

And if that's not quite enough at the moment, well then, just go to the source. Put your backside up to that stove, and when that side is done just right, do the other side. Now you're talking warmth.

Somewhere, there's a birch tree. It's a young thing now, about as big around as your forearm. But it's going to grow. Its branches are weaving their purple tapestry against the winter sky now, but come summer those twigs are going to sprout little toothed leaves.

The rain is going to fall, and that tree is going to put on another couple of feet, and it's going to take on a little girth. Then October will strip it, and January will whip it, and the cycle will start all over again.

One day, when the time is right, somebody will fell that birch, and somebody will cut it up, and somebody will split it. Then some distant December evening, I'll stir the coals in my woodstove and toss in a chunk of that birch.

Then I'll go upstairs and find that sweet spot on the livingroom floor.

Dog Tired

The hill beyond this checkpoint is steep. It begins at the highway and climbs for maybe a hundred yards.

Halfway up the snowpacked trail, John Patten's 10 dogs had stopped. It was early afternoon about 40 hours and 230 miles into the 400-mile John Beargrease Sled Dog Race on Minnesota's North Shore of Lake Superior. The race is run annually from Duluth to Grand Portage and back.

The day was warm. Cars and trucks hissing by on the highway below had turned the snow trail across the highway to mush. The sun was shining, glinting off Lake Superior's ruffled surface.

"C'mon. Let's go," Patten said to his dogs.

He wasn't yelling. He was talking, trying to put enthusiasm into something the dogs weren't at all excited about.

Patten was alone, but a crowd of about 30 onlookers had gathered across the highway below. Some of them winced as they watched Patten struggling. Already he had been there for 10 minutes, coaxing, pleading.

"They've got it physically. They're just bummed," Patten said of his dogs.

Some were sitting. Some were lying down. A few were standing. Not one was pulling.

Patten had rested them for 45 minutes at Tofte, a small town just down the hill, but now the dogs were telling him that wasn't enough.

"It was just one dog, then it spread," Patten said.

He began tugging on the gangline, pulling each set of dogs forward, two by two.

"We're gonna do it the inchworm way," he told his team. "C'mon. Good dogs."

Patten wore no hat. His curly black hair was wet with sweat. His bib ties were loose on one side, sailing in the wind. But he was composed. If he was exasperated with the dogs, with this situation, he wasn't letting on.

He rubbed his dogs. He lifted them to their feet.

"OK, Johnny," he said. "Up there, buddy. C'mon, Gunther, Ranger fella. OK. Ready? On your feet."

But as soon as Patten left them the dogs slumped back to the ground. He had gained maybe 25 feet hauling his dogs forward. It seemed to be getting easier, pulling them, he said, so he got on the sled again. Mustering his most enthusiastic voice, he hollered at his lead dog. "Jack. Jack!"

Nothing.

Patten hung his head over the sled's uprights for several moments. Then he looked up, walked up to Jack and bent over. He dropped to his knees. Holding his hands away from the dog, he put his head to Jack's ear.

The dog yelped. Patten stood up.

"I bit his ear, if you're wondering," Patten said to the only observer present.

"Jack, I want you to pull," he said.

Jack leaned. No other dogs moved.

All of this seemed to last forever. The crowd below stared up the hill. Patten couldn't help but feel their eyes on his back. He was the race's defending champion. He was, at this moment, whether he liked it or not, a representative of the long-distance mushing community to all those looking on from below.

A trail official from above, where the trail leveled out, offered assistance. Patten accepted it. Together they pulled the team up the hill. The sled followed, like a toddler's blanket. It made no sound on the snow.

Patten had hoped that getting the dogs on level ground would be enough to get them moving. It wasn't. The animals simply stood there, casting motionless shadows across the trail.

One by one, they lay down. Patten didn't try to get them up. He started kicking snow loose from along the trail, tossing it on the dogs' backs and rubbing it into their groins to cool them.

"You try to get it where they don't have much fur," he said.

Patten took Ranger out of the team and began walking him back to the checkpoint. Ranger had diarrhea. Patten shuffled along like a soldier who was walking wounded.

"The race is over for him," Patten said of Ranger. "Maybe for all of us."

Four other teams had left the checkpoint ahead of Patten. Three more had passed him during his struggle.

After returning Ranger to the checkpoint, Patten got a can of 7-Up from his truck, then began the long walk up the hill.

At the top, he looked at his dogs. All were lying down. Most had their eyes closed. None moved when Patten returned. Snow was melting on some dogs' heads. Droplets of water clung to their fur. Patten sat down in his sled basket. He sipped the 7-Up.

"You know, sometimes nature tells us when to let go and leave it alone," he said, mostly to himself. "It's really tough mixing the two. You're really dealing with nature, and then you throw in this invention of man's called competition."

He reflected on that for a moment. Then he took a bite out of a Cheerio necklace he was wearing.

"Not bad," he said.

He would have plenty of time to munch and sip. He planned to rest there for a couple of hours, waiting for his dogs to recover.

"If they start waking up and standing up, I'll water 'em and go," he said.

The last time anyone saw him there, he was lying back on his sled with his Sony Walkman headset on. He didn't say what he was listening to.

Cold Feat

Most scientists agree that the lowest temperature ever recorded on Earth was 127 below zero near the Pole of Inaccessibility on the Antarctic ice cap.

But then most scientists have never stood and watched Duluth's Christmas City of the North Parade.

It isn't a matter of sheer temperature, you understand. The cold here is compounded by such factors as (a) lack of food, because the parade occurs at dinner hour; (b) the wind-tunnel effect of downtown buildings; and (c) knowing you really must find a public restroom soon but putting it off because your niece's drill team should be coming by any moment now.

This is to say nothing of that two-year-old swaddled at your side whose lips have just turned the same color as a mercury-vapor light.

But you don't have to suffer. You want to stay warm at the World's Northernmost Exhibition of Exposed Drum Majorette Legs? Try this:

Number One. Eat supper early. Get some calories in

that body. Soup with some backbone to it. Some bread. Maybe a pasta dish. You have to put fuel in the furnace.

Number Two. Forget fashion. "I freeze my [*bleep*] off every year at that parade," a local professional woman said.

"What exact part of your [*bleep*] do you freeze off?" she was asked.

"My feet," she said.

She freezes her feet because she wears normal, decent-looking "winter" boots. The R-factor of insulation in those boots is designed to get you from your well-warmed-up car to your climate-controlled mall. That's about it.

If you want to stay warm at the World's Northern-most Exhibition of Exposed Drum Majorette Flesh, you have to dress ugly. We're talking Sorels or equally insulated pac boots. The ones that make you look like a cartoon character going ice fishing. Go ahead. Look like a Minnesotan. It feels good.

And don't cram so many socks into those insulated boots that your toes get squished. If you can't wiggle your toes freely, you can't stay warm. That blood has to have somewhere to go.

Now let's work right on up your body. Legs: Wear long underwear. Maybe two pairs. No one will be counting. Sure, long johns look weird with a skirt. Don't wear a skirt. Especially if you're a man. Wear pants, preferably wool pants. The thicker the better. You have a downhill ski outfit? Wear it over the wool pants.

On top, wear the heaviest coat — or coats — you can wear. One, two, three of 'em. You know those Kelly-green Windbreakers, the ones that have words like "Jimbo's Lounge and Truck Stop" on the back? The ones they call "insulated" because they have a flannel lining? Don't wear one of those. They are made for people who want to be comfortable in the blue haze of Jimbo's Lounge and Truck Stop.

If you have only one coat, wear a couple of sweaters under it. If you have long-john tops, wear them. Yes, you'll look fat. But remember, you're not in the parade; you're just watching it.

Other trouble spots: hands and ears. Don't wear gloves; wear mittens. Or wear gloves under your mittens. You need something with insulation and something with some shell material (canvas, nylon) that will combat that wind-tunnel effect.

Stocking caps are great for heads, bad for ears. They always ride up and leave lobes exposed. That's what freezes. Either wear a scarf to cover your neck and ears, or wear something with ear flaps. With the flaps you'll look like a basset hound. Who cares?

Got a hood on your coat? Don't be macho — put it up and tie it.

The same advice goes for the youngsters. They're ahead of the game because they're either young enough to wear snowsuits — the ultimate warm garment — or they're old enough to enjoy dressing ugly.

But don't expect their feet to stay warm in those cute little snow boots. Sorels come in tiny sizes.

Another problem for kids is wrists. Those poochy little mittens abut directly to those poochy little snowsuit sleeves, but leave a gap. Solution? Slip a pair of thick, adult wool socks over their little mittens and up to their elbows. And don't fret about the nose drippings — just toss their socks in the laundry later.

That'll do it. Now get out there. Get ugly. Get warm.

Dorothy

Dorothy. Almost everyone just called her Dorothy.

They'd say, "We're takin' a snowmobile ride Saturday. Up to Dorothy's. Maybe do some fishin'."

Or, "It was almost dark by the time we got to Dorothy's."

Or, "This lady hopped out of a square-stern canoe and started wading up the rapids. It was Dorothy."

Of course it was Dorothy.

Dorothy Molter. The woman who lived — mostly alone — on a couple of islands in Knife Lake on the Canadian border. Dorothy died in December 1986. Natural causes, said U. S. Forest Service officials who found her. I suppose so. That's about the only kind of causes there are up on the Isles of Pines in Knife Lake.

I knew Dorothy a little bit. Stayed with her one time. Stopped by for tea a few more. Not that we were friends. You didn't have to be with Dorothy.

To be honest about it, we might have been better friends if I hadn't been a writer. She was wary of

writers, I think. Writers brought about too many inac-
curate headlines, one of which called her "The Loneliest
Woman in America."

That wasn't Dorothy.

She had a fence around her garden that was made
from the blades of paddles she'd received as gifts from
passing canoe groups. Nobody with that sort of fence
was lonely. Nobody who counted seven thousand sig-
natures in her guest book by summer's end was lonely.
Nobody who sold cold root beer for 35 cents a bottle in
the middle of the canoe country was lonely.

Nor was Dorothy a particularly colorful character.
She was a character, I suppose, simply because she lived
the way she did. But she wasn't a storyteller or a recluse
or someone who needed an audience.

She was just a good-hearted lady who reached out to
anyone who needed anything: a cup of coffee, a warm
supper, a length of rope, a bandage, or a needle and
thread.

It would be easy to glorify her, now that she's gone.
But it wouldn't be right.

It might, though, be worth considering the recollec-
tions of Jeff Davis, who as a kid from Duluth was
headed across Moose Lake east of Ely one winter day in
1956. He was 18, headed into the woods on a solo
camping trip.

"Then, in the distance, I saw another human figure —
you couldn't miss seeing that in winter — plodding
toward me, on snowshoes," Davis wrote. "It was
Dorothy.

"I didn't know then that anybody lived up there in
winter. I was really surprised when she drew close
enough and I could see she was a woman.

"Her hair was brown — dark — then. We stopped and
stood in our tracks for just a few minutes. Enough for

us each to introduce ourselves and for Dorothy to tell me about her home on Isles of Pines on Knife Lake . . ."

Dorothy went on to Winton to get supplies, Davis said. Davis spent a night in the woods and another night at Dorothy's cabin, where he was treated to supper and breakfast. He still remembers the baked ham and the Smucker's pineapple jam.

Bob Cary of Ely, Minnesota, remembers happening onto Dorothy the time he and some friends were hustling back from deer hunting on Knife Lake. They'd been caught in a blizzard and two-degree temperatures.

"We were at the end of the portage where the Knife River empties into Carp Lake," Cary said, "when we heard this motor. This was back when motors were allowed in that part of the Boundary Waters. But the sound was coming closer. We thought, 'What the heck, that motor's going the wrong way, going into the woods instead of out.'

"Out of the swirling flakes comes this lady wearing no more than a big wool shirt and no hat. The snow was piled up on her shoulders and head. She had about five Duluth packs full of gear and food. She was heading in for the winter.

"We asked her if we could help her carry some of her gear over the portage. She said, 'No, I don't need any help.' And she took off her four-buckle artics and tossed them into the boat. She had tenners on underneath. She rolled her pants up above her knees and started wading up Knife Falls.

"That was just the way she lived. Up until the last few years she was tougher than nails."

Tough. And kind and generous and self-sufficient.

That was Dorothy. Living the simple life. By herself. With the wind in the pines.

Spring

Oh, Canada!
Secret Lakes
Sharptail Dance
Old Black Hound

Oh, Canada!

The wind had whipped Pickerel Lake into a froth.

The waves weren't big yet, but some of them were breaking in modest whitecaps. We were quartering the chop in a 17-foot Old Town canoe. Every now and then a wave would send some splash over the gunwale and onto my legs. The water temperature seemed to be about 40 degrees.

Somewhere between an offshore island and the Canadian mainland, a fish seized Tom Klein's Thin Doctor spoon and began tugging. Klein, who was in the stern, had been trailing the lure as we paddled. He quit paddling and tugged back.

While I fought the waves, Klein fought his fish. The canoe drifted backward toward the island. Klein took up more line.

I tried to watch Klein over my shoulder. I wanted to watch. This was the first fish of our trip. The early May trip. The lake trout trip.

The wind gusted and the canoe bounced and Klein

pulled on his fish. Finally, it came up next to the canoe. Klein slid a hand into the cold water, grabbed the fish hard across the top of its back and lifted it out of the water. It was a three and one-half pound lake trout, lean and strong and wild.

Klein held it aloft and grinned.

"Canada!" he shouted into the wind.

I knew just what Klein meant. He wasn't talking just about the fish.

He was talking about the wind in his face and the smell of the air and the jostling of the canoe. He was talking about red pines and Duluth packs and distant islands. He was talking about rock and sky and water.

Canada.

Klein tapped the fish against the canoe thwart, picked up his paddle and got to stroking again. We regained the water we'd lost while he had fought the fish. By late afternoon, we were 10 miles down Pickerel on a jack-pine island where Klein had camped many times before.

The wind was still blowing out of the northwest when our companion Denny Olson came paddling up to camp that evening. Olson was to have come in with someone else, but those plans had gone awry. Undaunted, Olson had rented a solo canoe and come in alone.

"I needed this trip," Olson said.

Olson and Klein had happened onto this campsite in Ontario's Quetico Provincial Park a few years ago. They didn't think much of it at the time, but that was before they discovered the smallmouth bass and northern pike in a nearby bay. Bonanza Bay, they call it now.

The most remarkable fish ever produced by Bonanza Bay was a nearly 20-pound northern pike caught by a friend of Klein and Olson.

"Battlescar Galactafish," Olson said, remembering the monster.

If you go to Bonanza Bay with Olson and Klein, they will show you Galactafish Rock, where the big northern was taken. They still make morning pilgrimages to the spot, hoping.

But Bonanza Bay is a mere diversion from The Honey Hole, a dropoff in the main body of Pickerel that has given up lake trout in the nine-pound range. It is a 15-minute paddle from camp on calm water.

All of these fish — lake trout, northern pike and smallmouth bass — are legal to catch in this part of Canada as soon as the ice goes out. That is, ostensibly, why we had come here — to catch fish.

But Olson had gotten to the heart of it best. It had been a long winter. We needed this trip.

For two days, we listened to the wind hissing through the jackpine needles. We could get across the lake only once to fish The Honey Hole. It gave us three trout in an hour and a half, but nothing over four pounds.

Most of the time, we worked back in Bonanza Bay where the wind couldn't find us. One morning Olson and Klein returned to camp from sunrise fishing with northern pike of 10 and 12 pounds. No Galactafish, but mighty respectable pike.

On the third morning the wind stopped. Klein was already up and fishing in the bay from the solo canoe, a Mad River Slipper. Olson and I, waking later, took the Old Town.

The little bay looked primeval. Mist rose like torn wisps of cotton candy. A loon called. The sun was spreading butter on the pines.

It would have taken very little imagination to conceive of a time thousands of years ago when this bay looked exactly the same early one morning. The loon. The mist. The sun burning through it all.

We could see Klein across the bay, working the shoreline near Galactafish Rock. He looked good.

In our canoe Olson was in the bow, throwing a silver Cisco Kid at the shore. He wore wool gloves with no fingertips. We both wore several layers of clothes.

"The bass just aren't hitting at all on this trip," Olson said.

Which, of course, was the cue for a couple pounds of smallmouth to batter the Cisco Kid. The fight was quick. Bass don't fight like bass until the water warms up. Olson pried the Cisco Kid out of the fish's lip and sent the bass swimming again.

We caught and released a few more before we came up on Klein. He had caught several bass, including three with three casts at one point, he said. Like us, he was ready for breakfast.

The mist had burned off now. Ruby-crowned kinglets were gossiping in the woods. Somewhere, a grouse drummed.

"Hot chocolate's going to taste good this morning," Olson said.

Back at camp, the smelt went in the channel before the bacon and eggs went on the griddle. We always fished from camp, paddling dead smelt out from shore by canoe, dropping them on the bottom. Someone on shore would jam a rod in some rocks, and we'd wait for the lake trout to come along.

Breakfast was still cooking on the campstove when Olson bolted for his Daiwa Mini-spin fishing rod. The rod is one of those suitcase jobs. Cute little thing. Ultralight rod. Baby spinning reel. Six-pound-test line.

At the moment, the rod was curved in 90-degree arc,

pointing at a riled up lake trout. Olson grabbed the rod and set the hook.

"This may be the one," he said.

Klein and I stood nearby, waiting. We had heard that kind of talk before.

"This one feels good," Olson said.

We had already caught a few fish this way. Three or four a day, all of them three or four pounds.

The delicate spinning reel whined when the trout made a run. Olson just smiled. When the fish finally tired, Olson coaxed it ashore and Klein pinned it on a rock. The lake trout was a six-pounder.

"Now this is the way they're supposed to be," Olson said.

He put the fish where it wouldn't go anywhere. Then we got back to our bacon and eggs.

Another morning found Klein and me working the shallowest part of Bonanza Bay. It was back where the bay became a finger, where a small trickle of water came in from some beaver ponds.

"I'll play guide here," Klein said. "You just fish."

I was tossing a fluorescent orange jointed Rapala, which looks nothing like any minnow I've ever seen before. But it keeps catching fish, so I keep using it.

A couple of casts at a loaf-of-bread rock produced nothing. I had almost run out of things to cast toward, but I tossed the floating plug at a brontosaurus-spine rock.

Something happened beneath the water. It wasn't far from the canoe. A thick, green body swirled. I wouldn't have wanted to be down there. The fish was scary big. Klein saw it, too. I hung on to my little graphite rod.

I suppose I set the hook. I don't really remember. The little reel talked, and the big northern walked. He didn't come out of the water, just pulled the canoe around for a while, thrashing occasionally. Klein, ever the guide, wouldn't let the fish get too close to a confusion of timber under the water.

The fight wasn't long, but I remember my arm being tired. I remember wondering just how to handle a northern that big. He would surface, slowly, out away from the canoe. His back was black and gleaming and too broad for one hand.

Then I had a good idea.

"You want to land him?" I asked my guide.

My guide said, "I'll land him for you."

We hadn't brought a landing net. That would have been too easy. So Klein grabbed the fish just behind the gills — not in them — and hefted him out of the water.

Fourteen pounds of northern pike hung dripping over the water. We called the fish "Bob," which was a slight to a fish that was no doubt a female. We put Bob on the stringer for a while; we all have a little ego to massage. She posed for a few pictures with us.

But it wasn't long before Bob was swimming free again, back where she could join the other legends from Bonanza Bay.

We didn't often have calm waters on the trip, but at least we had the moon. One night some cumulus were riding the horizon, so the moon didn't appear until well after we'd finished a late dinner.

Klein was back in camp doing dishes. Olson and I had walked out to a gently sloping rock point. From the rock we had an unobstructed view of the main body of Pickerel, the clouds and the moon.

The moon was scattering silver on a corrugated lake. Olson and I weren't saying much, just standing, looking, listening to the water lap the rock. The night was as dark as a full moon night can be.

I'm not sure how long we'd been standing there when we heard the sound. It was a rushing of air, intermittent, like someone working a pair of bellows. Wingbeats. They sounded close.

I never saw the wings they belonged to, but Olson did.

"Loon," was all he said.

We stood there for a few moments longer, drinking in all that quiet. After a time, when the moment seemed sufficiently savored, Olson took a deep breath.

"I can handle it," he said.

Then we moseyed on back to camp, casting moonshadows on the rocks.

Secret Lakes

I have this friend. He's a fisherman.

He lives on the fringe of the canoe country, and he spends a lot of time on the lakes up there. He has lots of "secret lakes." Like lots of anglers do.

A secret lake — to an angler — is a lake that he or she has never seen anybody else fishing. Secret lakes are on maps. Some of them even have names. But as long as you never see anyone else fishing on one of these lakes, it's a secret lake.

My friend — we'll call him Spinner Bait — had a rough day this spring. Spinner Bait headed into one of his lakes for a little lake-trout fishing. On his first secret lake, he encountered six other canoes. All with two fishermen each. All of them fishing.

Bait was unhappy, to say the least. He even knew a couple of the anglers. One was an old friend. Didn't matter. Bait couldn't bring himself to fish in that kind of traffic.

So he paddled up a creek and through a couple more

lakes to another secret lake. Whoa. There was a canoe on that one, too. Another friend of his.

I don't know if Bait did any fishing that day or not. It might have been too much for him.

I know how he felt. A couple of springs ago four of us paddled into a little lake-trout lake in Ontario's Quetico Provincial Park. This was only a week after ice-out. The lake was six portages in. We saw no tracks on the portages. The whole wilderness was ours. It was ours — until we got to our lake, and found two other anglers already there.

Hard to say who was more disappointed — we or the other two fellows. We managed to fish the lake for a couple of days without tangling lines. But it wasn't quite the same. We thought it would be "our lake."

That's the whole thing, right there. A mutual friend was talking about Bait the other day. Said the friend: "He really thinks those are his lakes."

All of us know, on some level, that these lakes belong to anyone who wants to paddle far enough or pack in enough gear to live there for a few days. But not many people do it, and so, as often as not, we find ourselves alone in there.

And we catch fish. That's when we begin to get possessive. No one gets protective of a lake full of small northerns. But put enough three-pound walleyes or four-pound smallmouths or five-pound lake trout in there, and you've got yourself something worth coveting.

My wife, Phyllis, doesn't understand this secrecy business. She thinks we carry it way too far.

I know of this little bass lake up in the Quetico. I would never say the name of the lake out loud. You never know who might be listening. Phyllis scoffed at that. She even told a neighbor about the lake. I howled.

"Oh, he'd never go in there," Phyllis said.

She just didn't understand. Until one night last summer, when we found ourselves up on that little lake. It was just at twilight. We were the only ones there. The only ones, that is, except for about 75 smallmouth bass.

We dropped jigs. We flipped spinners. We cast minnow imitations. Didn't matter. These fish were lonesome and hungry. A few of these lonesome, hungry fish weighed four pounds. A couple of them wound up on the end of Phyllis' line.

Somewhere amid all the frenzy — not long after a four-pounder had been released — Phyllis turned to me and said, "We can't tell *anybody* about this lake."

I smiled, and got back to casting.

Sharptail Dance

A predawn wind stirs across the Wisconsin prairie. With the breeze, comes a distant honking.

"Geese," someone whispers in the dark.

The sound is a good one. It conjures up the image of a pothole full of big Canadas — some swimming, some walking the shore on their big black feet, some preening. Getting ready for another spring morning.

But we haven't come to see geese, and we hurry on.

Down the dirt path. Across the prairie stubble. Into the blind.

Through two slits in the canvas blind we are looking at a tiny patch of the 30,000-acre Crex Meadows Wildlife Area near Grantsburg, Wisconsin. This isn't just any patch of prairie.

This is where the sharptail grouse dance.

They dance here every morning from before dawn until midmorning or later, from late March until mid-May. If you are lucky enough to reserve a blind, if you don't mind rising at 4:30 on a frosty morning, and if you make your approach on quiet feet, you will see the dance.

And you will never forget it.

We do not see the grouse arrive. Suddenly, in the gray half-light, they are just there. Twenty feet in front of us.

Understand, now, these are not the ruffed grouse of northern Minnesota and Wisconsin. These aren't the grouse you hear drumming off in the woods while you're out fishing. These are their prairie cousins, found in upland cover where the aspens and birch give way to brush and grasslands.

Sharptails are about the size of chickens. They have the buff coloring of a hen pheasant, except for a white patch under their tails. In short, they are an average-looking creature — until they begin to dance.

Then the tail goes straight up toward the sky. The wings flare out and curl down to the ground. The bird's head is thrust forward, and a patch above its eye un-furls, revealing a canary-yellow strip the size of a sunflower seed. Finally, a walnut-sized sac appears to inflate on the bird's neck and takes on a pulsating purple cast.

That's just the video.

The audio is part turkey gobble and part dove coo — a throaty, chortling sound that seems to come from inside the bird rather than out its beak.

Then there's the strutting. The sharptails zip around, stomping their little feet up and down so fast they blur. All that stomping on the prairie sod runs together and creates a subtle buzzing.

With heads stuck forward and wings in hover mode and tails erect, the birds scoot around. The effect is that of a bunch of little wind-up airplanes taxiing about, looking for runways they never find.

It is only the males who do the dancing in sharptail social circles. The females are somewhere nearby, out of sight, watching all of this. Once moved, they fly in, mate with a male of their choice, and leave.

At first, peering through the slits in our blind, we think the birds are just running around helter-skelter. But after watching for a while, we can see that each bird is defining his own little territory. The territories may be only a few feet across, but each bird knows where his ground stops and his neighbor's starts. If he forgets, his neighbor quickly reminds him with a puffy — but nonviolent — confrontation.

As if choreographed by some unseen director, the birds all coo and strut for 30 seconds or so, then idle down. After a quiet period of about 15 seconds, they go at it again.

Often the birds seem to dance in pairs, facing off on territory lines, zipping back and forth in unison.

Meanwhile, as morning breaks over the meadows, geese begin to move out to grassy fields to feed. Sandhill cranes go creaking across the new day. From somewhere in the weeds comes a bittern's slough-pumper call.

The sun is up now, melting the night's frost. The sharptails don't seem to notice. They continue their dancing.

Suddenly, a pair of broad wings slice the air over the dancing grounds. A shadow, a dive — a hawk. Not just any hawk. A peregrine falcon. He swoops on the sharptails, who freeze or flush. The peregrine follows one of the sharptails that takes flight, but only half-heartedly. When the sharptail lands, the peregrine cruises on, and finally disappears.

Surely, capable of speeds up to 200 miles per hour, the peregrine could have had a sharptail breakfast if he had wanted one. Maybe he was just practicing.

One by one, within a minute, the sharptails all return. In a moment, the ground is astir again.

A minor distraction, that brush with death. The dance must go on.

Old Black Hound

Old Dave is fading. I'm afraid he won't be around much longer.

He can't hear a lick. Climbing three stairs to the back porch takes about all the gumption he can muster. On our walks, his pace is getting slower every night. And he was slow before.

Dave is the non-hunting, good-loving black hound who came into our lives about 14 years ago. He looks mostly like an Irish setter that got dipped in used motor oil. But he never knew that, and he always carried himself with a certain jauntiness.

Dave was a bargain. We rescued him from doggie death row at a humane shelter in Kansas. He could have been a K mart Blue-Light Special at $7.50.

In the early years, Dave was all legs and curiosity. We lived in the country then, and I remember taking him for a run with me one night. We were a couple of miles from home when we passed a rural school. Someone was conducting a dog obedience class in the schoolyard.

Dave was not what you'd call long on obedience. That was my fault, not his. When Dave looked over at that schoolyard and saw several rows of dogs sitting compliantly beside several rows of masters, he couldn't resist. Last time I looked, he was running up and down the rows, smelling the whole class. I picked up speed and moved on. He was still there when I went back with the car to pick him up. That was no problem: He'd always get in the car.

The car always held a spell over Dave. In the summer, if we'd left a window down, we might look all over for the boy, only to find him curled in the passenger seat up front. He just wanted to be ready in case anyone was leaving.

Somewhere along the way, we moved north, and Dave rode right up front in the U-Haul 24-footer. He came to know mosquitoes, blackflies and snow that balled up between his pads.

Dave was always exciting to have along on a canoe trip. In the canoe he was kind of like having an extra Duluth pack that moved. Phyllis and I were fishing on a little rainbow-trout lake once, and Dave was observing from his nest just ahead of me in the stern.

He got all worked up when Phyllis tied into about a two-pound rainbow. I landed it for her and was attempting to get a blue Rapala out of the fish's lip. A Rapala comes with two sets of treble hooks on it, or six hooks in all. Dave swooshed his shaggy tail, and suddenly the fish, the Rapala, my hands and Dave's hindmost extension were one.

Every time the fish flopped, Dave would jump. Every time Dave jumped, the fish would go nuts. Every time either did anything, I'd jerk my hands out of the way. It was quite a scene. Somehow, Dave avoided an impaled tail, I escaped a hooked hand, and the fish tasted good at dinner.

Nothing was ever routine when Dave was along. But he wrote equally bizarre scripts when we left him home.

Once we left him at home for an evening during the Christmas holidays. We made sure the trash was out of his reach, so he wouldn't inspect it, which he'd done on many occasions.

When we came home, it looked as if Dave had had a quiet night to himself. It was sometime the next day when we noticed the hooks and strings lying on the floor near the Christmas tree. Dave had found three gingerbread cookie decorations too much temptation, and we had hung all of them high enough that we thought they were out of his reach. I'd have given almost anything to see the skinny guy standing on his hind legs nibbling those cookies off that tree.

Dave's dining was legendary — at least in the family. He once devoured an entire loaf of bread dough we had put out to rise. I was afraid it would keep rising in his stomach and he'd explode, but the veterinarian said not to worry.

Once when we were out of town, a friend took Dave to visit some friends in the country. Dave ate one of the friend's chickens. It was the kind of chicken that still had feathers on it. We always felt bad about that.

Maybe the best Dave dining incident happened one Thanksgiving weekend in Duluth. Our neighbor boy, Mark, showed up at our back door with Dave on the leash.

"Dave must have gotten loose," Mark said. "He was down at our house."

We thanked Mark for bringing Dave home. Mark

sort of hemmed and hawed for a moment, looking at his feet. Then he looked back at us.

"Yeah, he ate a pumpkin pie my dad had set outside to cool," Mark said.

I've always been sort of grateful that Mark's dad didn't come over and beat me up. I tried to apologize to him, and he tried to be kind about it. Then I went out and bought a frozen pumpkin pie and delivered it to Mark's family, but I'm sure their Thanksgiving meal wasn't quite the same.

Dave seemed thirsty the rest of the afternoon.

It's been a while now since Dave has pulled any fast ones. The only time he runs now is when he's lying on the kitchen floor, asleep, chasing rabbits in his dreams. His feet flinch. He whimper-barks. Those rabbits are in big trouble.

I'm not sure how much longer Dave will be harassing those rabbits. I don't think I can wait until he fades away on his own. I think that would be too painful for both of us.

But someday, when the time seems right, Dave will make The Long Portage. I hope there's a pumpkin pie waiting for him when he gets to the other end.

Summer

Nothing Doing

A halfhearted shower was falling when I pulled in at the Scandia Bakery. The bakery sits right on the highway at Schroeder, Minnesota, on the North Shore.

I have tried to drive past the bakery before, but the car always seems to know. It veers over anyway. I have no choice.

I needed some trail food, I figured. Something like a sugar doughnut and a caramel roll. Back in the car I drove on toward Canada, chewing to the beat of the windshield wipers.

I wasn't sure where I was going. I had left Duluth about 8:30 in the morning. I had tossed a few things in the car I thought I might need — daypack, wool shirt, matches, compass, paddle, life jacket, rain gear.

It had been a couple of weeks since I'd been in the woods, and I needed to get out there again. I needed to see what the bugs and the birds and the blossoms were up to.

It wasn't easy for me to go wandering so aimlessly. The night before, I had fought off the urge to call someone up the Shore and line something up. That would have been against the rules. You can't very well wander aimlessly if somebody is expecting you.

The sky was still spitting when I pulled over at the Cascade River to inspect a roadside outhouse. After the inspection I happened to notice the trail leading upstream, along the river. I realized that in seven years of chasing up and down the Shore, I had never ventured up the Cascade.

I threw on the wool shirt, a rain jacket and the pack. I started walking.

Like most major North Shore streams, the Cascade ambles peacefully through the uplands. Then it plunges and crashes the last few miles through rock canyons and natural stairs to its rendezvous with Lake Superior.

The trail was good, and the air smelled as thick as it always does on damp mornings. While I went up, the river came down. It thundered white into a 15-foot shaft, boiled at the bottom, then turned back to root beer.

Long sheets of clear bubbles became elastic just before they slipped over the next drop. I could have watched them all morning.

Along the trail a profusion of bunchberry did some cascading of its own. It was draped on both sides of the trail, showing off its white blossoms. The bluebead lily was about to blossom, too, and the balsam fir boughs had put out the delicate green needles of the new summer. It's a short season, this time of growth. Short, and worth savoring. I descended and wandered on up the Shore.

I knew a canoe outfitter in Grand Marais, and I stopped there to pick up a solo canoe. I wandered up the Gunflint Trail north of Grand Marais to a little river. A friend had told me about the spot a couple of years before. People see a lot of moose there, he'd said.

It's where the Brule River flows into Northern Light Lake, about 12 miles northeast of town as the heron flies.

I tossed my gear in the canoe and paddled downstream, pushed by a westerly wind.

I wanted very much to see a moose. I wished I had been paddling at dawn instead of early afternoon, but when you're out wandering, you have to accept those things.

It was only a mile downstream to the lake. Four goldeneyes whistled past me. They looked like drakes. Then I noticed a hen along shore, farther downstream. She wasn't going to fly, so I thought I'd paddle over for a visit.

Should have figured it. She was a mama goldeneye. I didn't know that for sure until I saw 11 little goldeneye fuzzballs plopping into the river from their sunning log.

Mom clucked to them and scolded at me. I took a couple of pictures, thanked her, and apologized for the intrusion. Then I went moose hunting.

I poked around a moosey bay of Northern Light Lake until I was sure no moose were sauntering along the shoreline. I was a little disappointed. About as disappointed as you can be paddling a canoe on a perfect summer afternoon in the finest country anywhere.

When I paddled back up to the boat landing, I met a couple of fellows sliding an aluminum boat into the water. They were going fishing. One fellow wore a forest green jumpsuit, the kind that zips up the front.

"See anything?" he asked.

I thought he meant fish. I told him I hadn't fished.

"I saw the camera. I thought you were looking for moose," he said.

I told him I was and had struck out.

"One night, summer before last," he said, "we counted our twenty-fourth one right here at the landing. Didn't we, Wayne?"

Wayne, hauling a 6-horse Evinrude down to the boat, nodded.

Twenty-four moose. Even if Wayne and his buddy were counting the same ones twice, that's a dozen. I made a note to come back some evening.

When I rolled back down the Shore, it was getting on toward suppertime. I had to fight the urge to hustle on home. I had one more piece of territory I wanted to see. I stopped at the Cascade Lodge and had a piece of strawberry-rhubarb pie to slow down. The ice cream helped, too.

This last stop was like an old friend. It was the Oberg Mountain hiking trail near Tofte. The Oberg loop is just a two and one-half mile hike, but it's kind of like walking around the crown of a 10-gallon hat. From up on Oberg Mountain you can see forever. Forever south and east is Lake Superior blue. Forever north and west is what we Minnesotans affectionately call the Sawtooth Mountains.

They're just good hills, but somewhere down near the brim of that hat lies Oberg Lake, a sapphire of a pothole. It's nothing much by itself, but when you look at it from up so high, you feel you have just created the world, and it turned out just the way you wanted it.

Then I saw the bear, right on the trail, about 20 yards away, looking at me. He saw me the same time I saw him. He wheeled and bolted, disappearing into the maple forest.

It wasn't a big bear. In fact, it was small enough that I

wondered if his mother was nearby. Which got me thinking about all kinds of other things.

Like the claw marks I'd seen on one of the wooden signs near an overlook.

Scared? I wasn't scared. I call it a heightened sense of awareness. Yeah. That's all it was. But it sure made me walk fast.

I didn't see any more bears the rest of the hike. What I saw were black insects. They looked like beetles and were an inch or so long. They were all over the trail, and, judging from their behavior, it appeared to be their mating season.

My insect book told me they might be creatures called May beetles, also called June beetles. I tried not to step on many of them, but it was tricky, what with watching for all the bears.

I treaded on back to the car and pointed it toward Duluth.

I'd had nothing to do, and I'd done it. A person ought to do that more often.

Kayaks and Sails

No one is sure when the idea germinated. Like the boats themselves, the concept of the trip didn't just occur. It was built in stages.

"To me, it's kind of cloudy," Jeff Larson said. "It really started when we first started making the main hulls."

That had been the idea in the beginning. Larson, 37, and his friend Mark Hansen, 32, both of Grand Marais, each decided to build themselves a two-person kayak. The boats would be 80 pounds of Fiberglas and epoxy. Point to point, they'd stretch 17 feet, 10 inches.

But if you know anything about Larson or Hansen, you might have suspected the tinkering wouldn't end there.

So, it should come as little surprise that on a sunny Monday in late August, midday would find them on a cobblestone beach of Lake Superior near Grand Marais. Beside them were two kayaks, each rigged with a pair of 12-foot outriggers and a full set of sails.

That's right. Sails.

The trip would be a week long, cruising the North Shore, wherever the winds would take them.

"We were intoxicated with the idea of cruising the lake," Hansen said. "We talked about it all winter."

Then they coaxed a friend into joining them, which is how there came to be three of us on the pebbled beach that August morning.

Heaped in various piles and stuff sacks near the boats were sleeping bags, a tent, a two-burner Coleman stove, a gallon of fuel, thermoses of coffee, a week's supply of food, polypropylene long underwear, sweaters, jackets, rain gear, a wetsuit, boat cushions, life jackets, tarps, paddles, oars, two Sony Walkmans with headphones, several cassette tapes, repair kits, first-aid kits, two small coolers, a 2-horse Johnson outboard, six gallons of outboard gas, a MinnKota trolling motor, a 12-volt battery, bilge pumps, sponges and about 20 bungee cords.

Somehow, all of that was stashed fore, aft and mid-ship in the kayaks, with room left over for two of us in Hansen's boat and Larson in his own boat. In a northwest wind at about 10 knots, we shoved off.

Not everyone thought our journey was a wise one. A Grand Marais commercial fisherman had as much as told Hansen he was crazy.

We knew what the fisherman was getting at. These weren't 30-foot sailboats with six feet of weighted keel, the kind designed to ride out the worst Lake Superior can whip up. Furthermore, our sailing experience was measured in days, not years.

We hoped to offset our own inexperience and our crafts' liabilities by sailing close to shore and by sailing conservatively. Yet we acknowledged the risk.

"There's an element of danger connected with sailing,

especially here on the big lake," Larson said. "Here it can turn so fast on you, and the water's so cold.

"The potential for danger appeals to me — getting as close to it as you can when you still have control to get out of danger. It's thrilling to me. It's foolish to others."

Hansen looked at it differently.

"To me, I don't have any need to go near the edge myself, or to see what I can get away with," he said. "What I like to do out here is something more than reasonable, something modern man doesn't do much of anymore."

Respected or ridiculed, we were off.

To move with the wind is an adventure in silence. We were pushed along by winds that rode down over the Sawtooth Mountains and out over the lake, light winds that often had us wishing for more.

But then they would kick up ever so slightly, and suddenly we would be scooting along. It wasn't so much a sensation of speed. It was simply freshness on our faces and a more serious gurgling where the bow and the two outriggers cleaved the water.

It got even better than that when we were on the downhill side of a swell. These weren't large rollers. They weren't anything like whitecaps. They were an almost imperceptible lifting of the boat, and then, after a moment's hesitation at the top, an accelerated slide into the unseen trough.

When this happened, Hansen and I would look at one another and smile. Both of us felt it. That was enough.

Something about sailing makes you feel as if you're getting something for nothing — and you are. We weren't putting energy behind a paddle. We weren't putting gas through an outboard. We were just borrowing some air that happened to be going our direction.

One afternoon on a cobblestone beach, Larson tried to describe the sailing experience.

"You're in a different world, where . . ." And here his voice trailed off. "Boy . . ."

The waves nuzzled the shore and receded several times as he searched for the right words. Finally, he spoke again.

"I don't know how to explain it," he said. "It's kind of like what music does for some people. It's relaxing, yet thought-provoking. It brings on thoughts you don't get normally."

Said Hansen: "You're unattached to the regular world. You can cover some distance, and you can do it with a minimum of effort. It's free power."

All of that seemed to be intensified by the size of our boats. When the wind shifted, so did our weight. There were liabilities to sailing such small boats on a big lake, but there were assets, too.

We spent our first night on a gravel beach beneath the three-room home of Helmer and Chrestine Aakvik near Hovland. Helmer, 89, has fished the lake commercially for decades. Now he catches herring mainly for suppers.

Chrestine, 80, prepared us a supper of pancakes, real maple syrup, ham sandwiches, coffee and tea. The Aakviks are Hansen's friends. We sat around the kitchen table until the light had begun to fade in the west, talking about people of the North Shore, about the "good ol' days" of commercial fishing on the lake and about Helmer's first months in this country 70 years ago.

If Helmer thought our trip was crazy, he didn't let on.

Perhaps he, more than the others, understands what it is young men must do sometimes.

The wind was a whisper when we left Helmer's beach the next morning. He stood droop-shouldered and leaning on his cane, outside his home, watching us put in. Chrestine was at his side in her dress and sweater.

"I hope you get a breeze," Helmer hollered.

We're not sure how long they stood and watched us as we moved out onto the lake and caught just enough wind to disappear around the point.

Another day drifted by lazily, Larson and I in one boat, Hansen alone in his. We sailed when we had wind. We motored when we were in the doldrums, which was often.

"You know it's a bad sign when the mosquitoes can keep up with you," Larson said.

Larson and Hansen listened to the seafaring songs of Stan Rogers on their Walkman headphones. I read *Huckleberry Finn*. We pulled out a wooden seat platform and prepared our peanut butter and jelly sandwiches for lunch. We popped fun-size Butterfingers and Snickers bars in our mouths.

And we watched the shore drift by. It is considerably more pleasant to observe North Shore cabins and lake homes from a sailboat than to watch mailboxes and driveways from a car.

We weren't the only ones moving on this cloudy Tuesday. The great blue herons were migrating. We had seen 11 of them the day before, and saw about as many on this day. They would fly over the water in ones and twos, or occasionally in a group of four, flapping patiently, legs floating behind them.

At one point we also saw a group of about 20 cormorants moving south, flying in formation much like geese.

Contrasted with these natural events and the easy creaking of our boats was the highway. We could hear it during much of our first two days, the trucks barreling north and south, the cars hissing past, the bonking of crane-borne jackhammers at construction sites.

Toward evening, we made the crossing of Grand Portage Bay and rounded Hat Point. That put us in Waus-Wau-Goning Bay, a four-mile-wide expanse where we hoped to camp.

It isn't easy to select a campsite from two miles out on Lake Superior. We would study the shoreline through binoculars and see what appeared to be a suitable cobblestone beach. We would sail for it. Then, upon closer examination, we would see that it was cobblestone, all right, but that it ascended from the water steeply for four or five feet, making it impossible to pull our boats up.

We sailed for the farthest corner of the bay, where we saw another beach. This one, at least through the binoculars, appeared smooth enough to pull the boats onto. Our hopes rose. Getting closer, we could see the beach area was a thin strip along the water, crowded from behind by alders and willows. Our hopes fell.

All of this happens at a time of day when one is tired and hungry and eager to be on shore after 10 hours in tight quarters.

We cruised a mile or more of beach, looking for enough room for the boats and our tent. Nothing looked inviting. Finally, we went ashore at the most likely looking spot.

The beach was sand and egg-sized pebbles. Just wide enough to pull the boats onto. We scouted for a tent site. There, just beyond a horizontal cedar, was a flat spot. It must have been a campsite. Why else would someone before us have nailed a flat plank to the cedar tree to sit on?

We unpacked and made the place our home.

Camping on cobblestone beaches is clean camping. No sand gets in your food or your tent or your boots. No dirt works into your fingernails and the knees of your pants.

Then, too, there's the sound of cobblestone camping. Lying in the tent in the morning, you always know when one of your companions is up and around. A short trip to the fire sounds like someone walking in wooden shoes through a roomful of gumballs. No one sneaks up on anyone at a cobblestone beach.

Cobblestone beaches also come with a recreation program. Waiting for coffee water to boil? Skip some rocks. Larson set the record with an enviable nine-skipper. And how much time can three grown-up boys spend zinging pebbles at a floating stick with a slingshot like the one Hansen brought? About half an hour.

Shortly after Hansen packed away his slingshot on our third morning of the trip, we set sail for the Susie Islands. The Susies are a cluster of 12 rugged islands that lie a quarter-mile to two miles off the Minnesota mainland about five miles from Grand Portage.

One look at the Susies and you can almost feel the last glacier scouring its way over this country. They are, for the most part, finger-shaped juttings of rock oriented from northeast to southwest, shrouded much of the year in mist and fog.

It is this cool Lake Superior microclimate that makes the Susies unique. They harbor several species of arctic and subarctic plants that are uncommon anywhere else this far south.

Many of the islands' rocks look like some painter's jagged dropcloth, so spattered are they with lichens of orange, gray-green and black. In other places, moss eight inches thick carpets the rock almost to the water's edge. It hangs there, raw and rooty on the bottom where it has been chewed back by the waves of vicious northeasters.

It was on one of these north-facing hanging bogs that Larson discovered the small red berries. They grew with small twigs and leaves on the surface of the moss.

Larson plucked one of the berries.

"Throw that down the chute," he said.

I popped it into my mouth. It exploded next to my cheek. A cranberry.

"That is special," Larson said. "You don't find them that often."

We picked only a couple more, then took pictures of the rest. It didn't seem right to eat any more. These berries had worked too hard to live here.

That is the overriding impression of the Susies — that life is hard here. Nothing is given. Every brief moment in the living process is earned.

Caribou moss softens rock outcrops atop Susie Island, the largest of the cluster. Sphagnum carpets the low-lying areas so thickly it envelops boot tops. Old-man's beard, a shaggy lichen, makes old spruces look even older.

Near one shore Larson found the rare butterwort, a tiny plant that eats insects for a living. Attracted to its violet flower, the insects land on its sticky leaves and cannot escape. The leaf rolls inward to enclose the prey, and the plant digests it.

Life is tough — and slow — on the Susies.

We camped on a deserted cobblestone beach on Big Susie Island. For two nights around driftwood fires, we discussed lofty topics: Marriage. Kids. Living simply. Wilderness management. Vietnam.

If we needed more wood for the fire, we simply walked a few steps away, picked up more driftwood and tossed it on. It was everywhere.

One night, the Northern Lights came glowing over the blackness of the Sawtooth Range like some half-halo. The lake was flat, and it beamed back a mirror image of the Lights and the shoreline.

Somewhere off in the distance, an ore boat chugged down the heart of the lake. Its diesel drone carried for miles over the water, then reflected off the mainland a half-mile away back to our ears. The low vibration was just detectable, like some locomotive heard from the outskirts of a small town.

A pebble exploded in the coals.

Sometime, long after the Northern Lights had become a memory, we clattered across the cobblestones to bed.

Morning came riding a northeaster. The skies were the color of an ore boat's hold. Waves were breaking on what had been our peaceful little beach.

We were on the water by 8:30. Larson had furled his jib sail and Hansen his mizzen sail. We wouldn't need to borrow much wind today.

The plan was to use the protection of the Susies for as long as possible, then make the two and one-half mile crossing to Hat Point. Once around Hat Point, we could use it for protection as we negotiated Grand Portage Bay.

The lake had been making whitecaps during breakfast, but laid down just enough to erase the white when we left camp. Still, as he pushed off, Larson took the solid part of a wave into his cockpit and Hansen and I bounced the nose of our boat off a rock wall before we got underway.

But we were on the windward, eastern, side of the island. All was quiet on the western front. Through the binoculars we glassed the waves toward Hat Point. No whitecaps. Waves, yes. But no whitecaps.

"Whattaya think, Larson?" Hansen hollered.

"Let's get goin' before it gets worse," Larson yelled back.

We pointed our bows at Hat Point, which was rapidly fading in a fog, and let the wind nudge us away from the Susies.

The feeling was something like dropping over the lip of a rapids, except it took longer in coming. The farther we got away from the Susies, the more the waves built. Still, they were nothing to be concerned about.

Hansen and I were tucked under spray skirts. Hansen wore full rain gear and a pile cap, earflaps down. The temperature was somewhere in the 50s. The mist thickened. Some might have called it drizzle.

Larson, with more sail area, nosed ahead of us, bouncing on the foot-high waves. He, too, was wearing warm clothes, rain gear and a pile cap. Nobody was listening to Stan Rogers. Nobody was reading *Huckleberry Finn*.

Hansen wanted to cross the open stretch as quickly as possible. He left his sail up, open to the wind, and fired up the 2-horse Johnson. The little motor purred to life and kicked us past Larson, into the gray.

A mile or so out, the wind came up, ruffling the waves that had already built. ·

"I don't like this," I told Hansen.

He didn't reply.

The waves kept building. We were now halfway across the sweep of open water. Turning back would have been foolish. Sailing broadside to the wind and waves would have been more foolish. We were committed.

The closer we got to Hat Point, the rougher the water became. We remembered stories of water piling up on Hat Point, slopping back, creating a nasty chop just off the point.

The waves grew to three feet, then four. With the swells and the slosh off of Hat Point, it was a rough ride. We began to feel small. Very small.

Solid water broke over the bow of the kayak up to the edge of the cockpit, about two feet in front of my face. Solid water broke over the stern somewhere near where Hansen was resting his back. The slosh wanted to push the boat sideways.

"How you doin'?" I asked Hansen.

"So far, so good," he said.

Almost the entire length of Hat Point was now obscured by fog. Only the tip was still visible. The thought of trying to clear that craggy point in a fog was chilling.

But we were getting nearer the point every minute. The boat wasn't taking any water. The outriggers and bridging were holding up well against the forces of the water.

We had been on the open stretch for 40 minutes or more. It was a long time to be scared.

Then, finally, we bounced around Hat Point, and Hansen cranked the tiller. The rudder bit the waves and sent us scurrying around the rocks, onto the gentle swells of Grand Portage Bay.

I turned and looked at Hansen. We both smiled broadly. It had been a lot more ride than we'd bargained for.

We waited there in the lee until Larson came sweeping around the point. We gave him the thumbs-up signal. He gave it back.

I couldn't help thinking about some of the comments Larson had made earlier. About danger. About being on the edge. I asked him if he'd had enough of the edge for a day.

"I've had enough," he shouted back. "Enough for a month."

Maybe we were lucky. Maybe the big lake had been kind to us, taught us a lesson cheaply. Maybe we would sail differently in the future.

But something else Larson had said kept hanging in my mind, too.

"Maybe there has to be a little foolishness — calculated foolishness — for something to be thrilling," he had said. "There's a feeling inside you can't get any other way.

"If you want to live your life safe and stay in the house all the time or sit in the lawn chair — fine. But you wouldn't get that feeling. To me it's worth it to get that feeling."

The trick is not getting a month's worth in one day.

Northern Lights

I don't know what makes the Northern Lights. I remember reading the scientific explanation somewhere along the way. I just don't remember what it said.

I'm not so sure I want to know anyway. I prefer to think of them as magic. Or part magic, part Robert Service and part Jack London.

I saw them again this week. What a show. Great misty-green shafts shooting out of the northern horizon, like a battery of search lights run by a madman. Or a Fourth of July fountain you thought was spent, but suddenly sends two or three more bursts of light into the night.

It wasn't just the northern horizon. It was all over, and all the way to the top of the sky, if such a place exists, as if the earth were merely a baseball game, and the sky some pulsating domed enclosure.

When the Lights are cooking like that, it's impossible to watch them long while standing up. You must lie down on a slab of granite, a boat dock, a grassy pasture. That's the only way you can watch the whole show.

That's what I was doing when they began to whirl and swirl and snake across the sky. There — a horizontal lightning bolt. Now a fluorescent serpent. Then a rippling from one horizon to the other.

Don't bog me down with talk of protons and ions. This is mystical stuff. I'm mushing my way over the Dawson Trail . . . I'm building the fire that will save my life . . . I'm alone in a lonely land, missing the one I love . . .

I can easily remember the first time I saw the Lights put on a display of this intensity. Two of us had gone to the Baptism River one night to net smelt. The smelt weren't running, so we left the river, climbed a bluff overlooking the lake and rolled out our bags under the stars.

We cooked chicken over a fire, then lay back to enjoy the night. It was then we noticed the sky was alive and shimmering with the green glow. Lake Superior, riled by an east wind, was crashing ashore at the foot of the bluff. At first we spoke often, oohing and ahhing, eager to make sure the other had seen a particular burst or shape in the sky. Then, for long periods, we would say nothing, just lie on our backs, watching above and listening below.

Finally we went to sleep, but I remember waking several times in the night to see the light still cavorting in the sky. It seems as if the Lights worked their magic all night, though it might have been only for an hour or two. When I awoke again, dawn was breaking over the lake. From that morning on I've felt different about this country.

I'll admit that every time I see the Lights I wonder all over again what makes them happen. But that's where I leave it.

Some things are better with the wonder left in them.

It Was Home

We paddled slowly up to the island. We beached the canoe on a flat rock and stepped out on legs that had been folded too long.

"How's it look?" I asked Phyllis.

"All right. Nothing great," came her answer.

We were a pair of tired paddlers looking for a campsite on Antoine Lake in Ontario's Quetico Provincial Park. The afternoon was waning, and the sky hung over the lake country like a bad bruise. Rain hadn't fallen all day, but it looked as if it might any minute.

"What do you think?" she asked.

I suspect I was thinking about the same things she was.

Neither of us was especially taken with the site. The broken glass in the rock fire grate was ugly. So were the charred ends of logs that had been too big for the last fire. The only piece of ground that looked flat enough for the tent also looked as if it would laugh at our tent stakes: Solid bedrock lay just beneath a thin layer of Quetico soil.

An hour later we were preparing vegetable crepes over a spruce fire and watching loons swim past our island like floats in a parade. The tent was pitched taut but stakeless on its tiny platform, thanks to a few sticks and 26 stones. A stack of firewood lay next to the fire grate. Our spirits were on the rise, and our little campsite felt like home.

That kind of mood swing isn't uncommon in the backcountry. Choosing a campsite is a little bit like moving into a new home. It can seem a little cold until you make it yours.

Almost no wilderness campsite is just right. It might have a nice rock fire grate, but its tent site runs downhill. Or maybe it's a campsite that would accommodate a group of 10, but there are only two of you. Maybe it's a fine little island campsite, but firewood is scarce.

When it's late in the day and you've put a lot of paddle strokes behind you, you notice all those things. You're beat. You don't really want to paddle on down the shore to see what another site might have to offer. But you aren't excited by the prospects of pitching camp, either.

Those feelings begin to change as soon as you start to make the camp yours. Spruce up that fire grate. Toss those charred logs back in the woods. Cut and split yourself some good firewood. You might even want to break out some trail food or sunflower seeds or a little cool drink to tide you over until supper.

Get that tent up. Roll out those sleeping bags. Pull out the clothes bag and change out of those boots into some tennis shoes.

Now you're talking. Kindle that fire. Get some supper going. Smell it wafting out of that old black cookpot. Get that coffee water on the boil.

Sit back and take a look. Looks like home, doesn't it? Feels like home, too. Don't you like the way that red pine is silhouetted against the sunset? And the way the tent looks in the last, low rays of the sun? This is what you came for. Have another cup of that after-dinner coffee. Those dishes will wait.

What's happening now is that this campsite is becoming something worth remembering. No longer will it be just a dot on a map or a clearing in the woods. It will take its place along with other good camps in your packsack of memories. Every time you look at a map of the area, your gaze will linger on that tiny island.

You'll construct the campsite in your mind's eye. And, if this memory is like those of other camps, a few details will come back more clearly than all the rest: songs around the fire, the fresh walleye dinner, the thunderstorm that had you sitting up in your tent.

All of that will come with time. Meanwhile, you have to get up and break camp the next morning. You have to take down the tent that looked so good in the setting sun, pack up those bags, and leave some firewood for the next travelers.

Don't be surprised if you find yourself looking over your shoulder as you paddle away. That wasn't just a campsite. That was home.

Fall

Good Scents

The shot was long gone, and so was the bird. I looked down and caught the purple of the spent shell lying in the weeds. I picked it up. It was still warm, and I held its open end to my nose.

Few aromas are sweeter to this hunter's nostrils than that of a just-fired shotgun shell. On the surface it is simply the smell of burned gunpowder. But ask any hunter, and you'll find it is far more than that.

It is the crackling of an October morning, the purposeful weavings of a dog on strong scent and the throb of a bird on the rise.

For me it's also the first pair of leather boots I bought at Hughes Clothing back in Kansas, an old red Falcon station wagon parked near a hedge row, and a blue hooded sweatshirt.

Nothing takes you home like a good smell.

I don't know what it is about a scent that send you back, but nothing else reels in the years and puts you there in quite the same way. Music comes close — at least the music of adolescence. Old black-and-white photos have a certain charm about them. The taste of Mom's Boston cream pie evokes some memories.

But when I want to go back, I let my nose take me there.

I suspect all of us do this. A hunting friend of mine says the oozing smell of a good marsh puts him back beside his dad in the duck blind. Another friend says the smell of just the right kind of smoke takes her back to the old trash barrel at home on the South Dakota prairies. And if you can take a whiff of a crayon without being carried back to early childhood, you were brought up differently than I was.

I was thinking about all of this the other day when I happened to catch the pungence of some autumn grass. It must have had something to do with the cool in the air, because summer grass never triggers this particular memory.

Suddenly I was a sixth-grader playing tackle football on the grass outside of a grade school in Grand Island, Nebraska. Next thing I knew, I was airborne in my mind, the same way my scrawny body was whenever Ronnie Peterson tackled me. Ronnie was about three times larger than I was, and he delighted in tackling me not conventionally but by grabbing one of my spaghetti-noodle arms and swinging me like part of a carnival ride for a few revolutions before letting me fly. Now, when I smell fall grass, I feel Ronnie Peterson's big hands on my arm.

Scents seem to call up more memories during the changing of the seasons. Spring is rife with good odors — like white pine needles on a south-facing slope — simply because we have spent six months without smelling much of anything outdoors.

Fall offers the counterpoint to so many of spring's coming-to-life scents. Fall smells like a million tiny deaths: aspen leaves, cedar needles, withering ferns. If you grow up stalking whitetails in Wisconsin's North Woods, the smell of late November must be popple forests, long johns hung over a woodstove and an uncle's cigar smoke in the shack.

But I suspect no smell speaks more universally for the North Country than that of woodsmoke. It comes in at least a couple of flavors. One is the kind that wafts out of woodstoves and into the winter night in towns like Eveleth and Ely and Two Harbors. It is the kind enjoyed most, I suppose, by those who walk their dogs late on crystal nights when the snow sounds as if it's breaking under your boots.

The other brand of woodsmoke rolls up from carefully tended little fires that spring to life in the bush. You've smelled them at shore lunches and on ghosty mornings in the canoe country and under coffee pots on day fishing trips.

I suppose all of these fires smell essentially the same. Yet each time we kindle the little sticks to life, we're retrieving moments from campfires past — and putting scents away for years down the trail.

Camouflage

Sometime in the October morning, they will begin moving.

They will move from warm beds to cold pickup seats, from warm sleeping bags to cold canoes, from dry pavement to soggy sloughs.

They will be duck hunters.

You won't see the hunters, of course. They'll be wearing camouflage. You might catch a glimpse of a face here and there, or a pair of hands moving mystically in midair. Your ears might pick up the subtle flumping of their waders or the clunk of a paddle against aluminum. But that will be it. Duck hunters are sly and crafty.

For the past couple of weeks duck hunters have been getting ready. They have been rereading the fall flight projections. They have checked the anchor cords on their decoys. They have tuned up their duck calls — surreptitiously, of course, on solitary road trips or long dog walks.

But mostly, duck hunters have been buying things. Duck hunting requires more things than almost any other kind of hunting, and it takes most of a lifetime to acquire all of the duck-hunting things you need. By the time you get around to acquiring the last of the things you really need, most of the things you acquired early have worn out. The circle never ends.

Camouflage is big. Duck hunters, remember, wore camouflage before it began showing up at department stores in sizes like 3T. Duck hunters need camouflage parkas, camouflage insulating layers and camouflage gloves. They need camouflage gun cases, shell bags, netting, caps and folding stools. They need camouflage overbooties, face masks, overalls, chamois shirts, tape, boat cushions, life jackets, gaiters, doggie beds and decoy bags.

I have also seen camouflage cigarette lighters. I assume anyone with a camouflage lighter also smokes camouflage cigarettes. I wonder what the smoke looks like.

Next to camouflage things, what duck hunters need most is decoys. Mallard decoys, tip-up feeder mallard decoys, bluebill decoys, a couple of Canada goose decoys.

Check that. You don't want a couple of any kind of decoys. You have to have an odd number, like 37. And always put a lonely looking hen at the end of the set.

The odd number invites singles, you know. A friend of mine went to buy a couple of Canada goose decoys to fill out his decoy set. The retailer said, sure, but don't buy two. Make it one or three. Canada geese mate for life, he explained. That odd number means someone's available. My buddy bought three.

I always wondered why ducks made three passes over our decoys before they came in. I've finally figured it out. Takes 'em that many passes to get the decoys counted.

Duck hunters also need lots of shells. That is difficult to understand for those who spend much time around duck hunters. Duck hunters, especially duck hunters far from the duck blind, are exceptionally good shots. Even at ducks 60 and 70 yards away. Seems as if duck hunters wouldn't need many shells to shoot their ducks. And this is true.

But all duck hunters know what you need lots of shells for. Many duck hunters spend quite a bit more time buying camouflage gear than they do training their dogs. When a duck goes down, it isn't always easy to get the dog to go pick it up. The hunter has to psych the dog up, or at least show it where the dead duck is floating. This is done by throwing things that make a splash near the floating duck. And what solid, heavy object is most readily available when you're floating in the middle of a marsh? That's right. Shotgun shells. You don't think a hunter's going to throw a camouflage lighter out there, do you?

All of this might sound a bit farfetched. I happen to know it's true. I'm a duck hunter.

But you won't see me bustling around in the half-light Saturday morning. Nope. Not in my new camouflage parka you won't.

Showtime

The campfire was burning low, the way it often does when dinner is over and the dishwater has already been warmed. Every few minutes one of us would toss on a piece of split spruce, and the fire would make flames again.

We wanted to keep it going. The evening chill was coming on, and we'd have a lot of fire-staring time before we went to the tent.

It was just the two of us, as it usually is on these fall trips. Phyllis and I were several portages into Ontario's Quetico Provincial Park. The campsite was a granite fist that punched through Kasakokwog Lake toward the setting sun. Twenty-year-old jackpines clung to the camp's thin skin of soil.

The sun had melted behind a spine of spruce a mile or so across the bay. That was just before seven o'clock. Days get short fast in late September. Now the dishes were just about finished, and the food had been tossed back in its Duluth pack.

The lake, which had been shoved around by a northwesterly wind all day, was settling down now. You could still hear it glurp and blup against hollows of shoreline rock in a couple of spots.

The western sky was getting on toward a serious pale when Phyllis moved out on the point.

"Let's get ready for showtime," she said.

We both knew what she was talking about. It had taken us by surprise the previous night, but tonight we would be ready. The ducks would be coming any time.

We hadn't even found a comfortable depression in the rock when we heard the first wingbeats. They sounded like someone working a bellows faster than any bellows could be worked. We looked up. Seven of them, coming in low.

We couldn't be sure what they were, but they were big enough to be mallards and their wingbeats looked right. They disappeared against the forest across the bay, so we listened for their touchdown. Several seconds passed. I imagined the birds swinging low, looking for the spot in the big bay they knew was right. Then it came, the whispered sloosh of feet and bellies on the water.

Within a minute they were talking. They were mallards, all right, or blackducks maybe, quacking and clucking.

They were followed, within minutes, by more. Three of them. A dozen of them. Then a couple of other bunches we heard but never saw. We lost count somewhere around fifty. The sky was losing candlepower fast, and where before we had been able to make out dots of ducks in a reflection on the water we could now just hear quacking.

We thought maybe the show was over, until we heard a sound like someone shuffling cards inside a sleeping bag. Then they appeared. More mallards, twenty or thirty of them, making their final approach down the lake. And right behind them, honking a lonely honk, winged a single Canada goose.

The birds already on the water were calling, and the late-arriving ducks and goose knew right where to go. There was no tentative circling, no cautious second look. The ducks and the goose coasted straight into the sweet spot on the bay.

The various groups talked back and forth, and an occasional rush of wings spoke of rearrangement on the water.

We wondered where these ducks had come from. Kasakokwog wasn't the kind of lake that held resident ducks. It offered few weedy bays where puddle ducks like mallards and blackducks like to feed. We figured these ducks and the wayward goose had moved down from someplace farther north. Northern Ontario. Manitoba, maybe.

I suspect these ducks' ancestors have been using this lake for a few hundred years on their journey south. Just what it offers that is so different from a few thousand others nearby is beyond me. I suppose if I were a duck, I'd know.

When we were sure the show was over, we trudged back to camp and stoked up the fire again. We wrote in our journals and talked about the kinds of things people always talk about while staring into fires.

Sometime before the Northern Lights came out, we took one final stroll down by the lake. From out there, somewhere on that wet reflection of stars, came a quack, then silence. Then another quack. More quiet. Then a honk.

We stood there for several minutes, just listening. We figured it would be good sound to fall asleep to.

It was.

Wild Moose Chase

We called him Fred.

He was about six hundred pounds of bull moose, and he was standing a hundred yards from our campsite on Marshall Lake, slurping long strands of aquatic grass.

It was midday, about eighteen hours before Minnesota moose season opened.

If Fred was worried about the coming season, he wasn't letting on. He'd just stare at us in our canoes, then bury his muzzle in the 40-degree waters of the lake again. When he'd raise his head, another stringy piece of Marshall Lake salad would be dangling from his jaws.

We watched him for a long time, but not with any thoughts of looking him up once the season opened. Fred wasn't the kind of moose we were looking for. Nope. Not with those spindly antlers, one of which seemed to have been broken off.

Nope. We hadn't paddled two lakes into the Boundary Waters Canoe Area Wilderness north of Grand Marais to shoot a wimpy bull like Fred. We hadn't toted a week's worth of grub, packed in three tents and towed in an extra canoe to haul home an adolescent moose.

It was nice of him to hang around camp the way he did for two days. He provided some nice atmosphere. But we were looking for Fred's daddy, or his grandpa maybe.

There were four of us: Bob Hanson, Mike Furtman, Bill Rudie and myself.

Unlike most of the thousand other Minnesota moose-hunting parties, we had chosen to pack in and live among our moose as we hunted them. At our campsite on Marshall Lake, we were about seven miles west of the Gunflint Trail, where the South Brule River meanders through some of the moosiest marshes in the North Country.

Our only concern was that we might take a nice bull sometime the next morning and have to head home. We had come not only to hunt, but to feel the backcountry in mid-October. Without mosquitoes. Without other canoeists. Without leaves on the trees.

We wanted to be here for a while — three or four days. We knew the success rate in Minnesota moose hunts varied from eighty to ninety percent. Even with the sixty to seventy percent success rate among those who hunted the Boundary Waters Canoe Area Wilderness, we figured our odds were good. Maybe too good.

We were entitled to take one moose — bull, cow or calf. But we had decided to hold out for a bull — a big bull — for the first few days of our one-week season.

That evening, around a campfire that mellowed the 35-degree chill, Furtman was sipping coffee. He took his cup down from his lips, stared in the general direction of the fire, and said, "Wouldn't it be something to shoot a big bull moose?"

It was something all of us had been thinking about since we'd applied for our license in the spring. But now that we were finally here, the reality was striking us. We were moose hunting.

Fred wasn't the only moose we'd seen on the eve of the opener. We'd made a 200-yard portage into another lake — where our hunting zone began — and had seen two cows. We had surprised another cow in a narrows. She stood and watched us as we paddled toward her, then trotted off into the woods. When we got back to camp, there was Fred, still munching and slurping.

Near as we could tell, there were moose all over the place.

We set our opening-day alarms for 4:45 a.m. We awoke not only to their beeping and buzzing, but to the drumming of rain on the tent. A quick tent-to-tent conference revealed that none of us wanted to hunt in a 40-degree rain.

We spent opening day eating pancakes and bacon, drinking coffee, napping and watching raindrops dapple Marshall Lake.

By the next morning it seemed as if we'd been in camp a week instead of two days. We were itchy to hunt.

The morning began the way every morning would in our moose camp. Alarms beeping at 4:45. Writhing into polypropylene long underwear inside a sleeping bag. Boiling water for oatmeal by lantern light. Finding gloves and bullets and rain gear and granola bars and orange vests and life jackets by headlamp.

Then we'd walk down the portage, headlamps dancing in the dark. If you were in the lead of that procession and you stole a moment to look back, you might have thought you were a turn-of-the-century miner going off to work.

We paddled to the spots we had chosen to hunt. They all had names by now — Moose Wallow Narrows, Lac Creek Point, The Rub, Moose Berry Hill. We were getting to know the country. It was beginning to feel like home.

Fred's granddaddy didn't show that day, a Sunday. Furtman saw two moose — a cow and another that slipped into the woods too quickly to be identified. That was it.

Monday. A frosty morning. Twenty-eight degrees at 5:00 a.m. Steam off the oatmeal. Cold feet in the woods.

By 8:00 a.m. Hanson and I had had about all we could take up on Lac Creek Point. We had stood up to shake some circulation back into our feet when Hanson spoke in a whisper. "Cow," he said. "Don't move."

About a hundred yards down the narrows, standing shoulder deep in frosted cattails, was the most gorgeous cow moose one could ever hope to see. She was backlit by the rising sun, as were all those frosty cattails.

She must have known something was up, because she lifted her nose high in the air, trying to catch some scent. We could see intermittent clouds of her breath expelled from her nostrils. The breath, too, was backlit. It would glow silver-gray for a moment, then dissipate into the morning air.

The cow was standing maybe fifteen feet from the water. Mist was rising in willowy columns, hanging over the lake, casting a mystical veil over the entire scene.

The moose was silhouetted, and at first we couldn't tell which direction she was facing. Then she turned broadside and held her head high to sniff again. She must have stood there for five minutes, though she

never seemed at ease. Perhaps she was waiting for a
bull to walk out of the woods at that moment. Maybe
that was the presence she had been inspecting the air
for.

Because we, too, were waiting for the bull, we never
thought about shooting the cow. Well, we thought
about it, but we never considered it seriously.

Finally the cow sauntered off into the spruce again,
and Hanson and I got back to thinking about how cold
our feet were.

Down at Moose Wallow Narrows, high on a rock
outcrop, Furtman was sure a bull was about to appear.

"I could hear his footsteps," Furtman said later. "I
could feel 'em."

Then Furtman came to his senses.

"It was my heart beating," he said.

The misty-morning cow was the only animal we had
seen all day, on a day that was as perfect as they get in
October. That night, back at camp, we talked about
moose hunting.

"It's harder than I thought," Hanson said. "Not as far
as physical labor, but after scouting and paddling up on
'em so easy, I figured it would be easy.

"Cow hunting is easy. Bull hunting is a lot harder
than I thought it would be. It's probably as hard as
hunting a buck."

"Maybe harder," Furtman said, "because there's less
density. There'd be a lot more deer around where you
were hunting deer than there are moose here."

We were beginning to lower our sights some.

"I think my bull requirements have shrunken," Furtman
said. "No longer does it have to be a 60-inch (antler)
spread. If it looks like Mickey Mouse, that's okay with
me."

We set the alarms and went to bed.

Something must be said here about how often the chance for moose hunting comes around in Minnesota. The season occurs every two years. About 20,000 parties apply for the 1,000 or so permits available each season. Once selected, a hunter must sit out another five seasons before applying for a license again.

The next time anyone in our party will be permitted to apply is 1997. As slim as chances are of getting a license, hunters often figure Minnesota moose hunting is a once-in-a-lifetime experience.

Which worried us some on Tuesday. We saw not a moose. We saw more sign — droppings, antler rubs on saplings, saplings broken by rowdy bulls, tracks, trails. But not a moose.

By Wednesday we were hungry. Hungry to see a moose on the hoof. Any kind of moose. Bull. Cow. Anything.

Funny, but earlier we'd been talking about how tough it would have been to shoot Fred. After all, we'd sort of gotten to know him. He was our decorator moose. He made our moose camp look moosey.

By Wednesday Fred was in jeopardy.

"You're darn right I could shoot him," Furtman said.

Wednesday morning we split three ways. At 11:00, when I paddled over to Moose Wallow Narrows to pick up Furtman for lunch, his eyes were big.

"I thought I was gonna get one," he said. "I could hear splashing upstream, working its way downstream around that blind bend. I got my gun ready and was waiting when out came — four otters."

We paddled up to get Hanson and Rudie on Lac Creek Point.

"I thought we were gonna get one," Hanson said, "I was sittin' here and I heard splish, splash, splash from

around the corner. I got my gun ready. I was shakin' so
bad."

But around the corner he found nothing but more
otters at play. Probably some of the same rascals that
had raised Furtman's heart rate.

At the next portage we ate crackers and salami and
cheese, sprawling in the midday sun, sleeping under
blaze orange caps. We were surprised to see two other
hunters coming across the portage, toting their canoe.
They were camped three lakes away. Had been for six
days. They were desperate.

"We haven't seen a moose," one said. "This is getting
old."

The tamaracks that had been smoky gold on our ar-
rival were now more smoky than gold. It had snowed
on us twice, enough to cover the ground lightly one
night. Our food packs were getting lighter.

Early on, each of us silently had wished he would be
the one to bring down the moose. Now it didn't matter.
All of us said so.

Thursday. Another vintage October day. Sunshine
and 55 degrees. A light wind out of the west.

But mooseless.

Oh, we heard moose again. But as on other days,
they were moose that turned out to be only the gurgling
of a swamp creek, or the rubbing of two trees in the
wind, or the back of a cap rustling against a collar.

"Just one of these times, I want to hear crash, crash,
crash — none of this tiptoeing around," Furtman said. "I
want to see those willows across the creek quakin'."

We had begun to wonder who was being hunted.

"All the time we're out there, I feel like there's a moose
or two watching me," Rudie said.

Words like "wily" and "crafty" began to creep into our

moose conversations.

"I think they're a lot smarter than we think they are," Furtman said.

And somewhere, at some quiet midday pause, when the frustration was beginning to tell, Furtman said what all of us had been thinking privately.

"You know something?" he said. "We may go home without a moose."

We had agreed we would hunt for a couple of hours Friday morning and head for home if we didn't shoot a moose. Our season allowed us to hunt through Sunday, but, to be honest about it, we were ready to go home.

That is probably hard to understand unless you have risen at 5:00 a.m. for six days in a row, eaten oatmeal in the dark, trudged down the portage, paddled up the two riffles, sat until your toes were numb, walked on those cold toes trying not to break a twig, pushed your hand into piles of moose droppings to see if they were warm, stared at the same shoreline five hundred times, eaten countless caramels, heard fifty or so phantom moose, paddled down the two riffles back to camp, unloaded the guns and daypacks, eaten another noodle and freeze-dried beef dinner, and gone to bed at 8:30.

Hanson and Rudie headed for Lac Creek Point. I dropped Furtman off at the rocky point overlooking Moose Wallow Narrows. Then I paddled on up to a small bay at the end of the lake.

Usually, I would have paused at Furtman's rock to load my gun. But for some reason, I felt this morning that I would be imposing on his solitude. I left the gun cased and paddled on, solo in the 17-foot Old Town.

I saw the moose as soon as I rounded the point. It was still before dawn, legal shooting time maybe, but not fully light. The moose was a dark form against the lighter cattails of a small marsh in the corner of the bay.

I was 50 yards from the animal.

I hurried to uncase the .30-06 I'd borrowed for the trip. As I wrestled with the gun, I heard the moose sloshing away from me. My only hope, I thought, is that the animal will stop to study me before it disappears into the woods.

I pulled the clip of bullets from my pocket. I put it in the gun. I put it in again, right side up this time. I snapped the magazine shut. I worked the action of the Browning automatic to chamber the first shell. It sounded quietly solid.

I looked up. The moose was gone.

I scanned the shoreline, trying to see a horizontal form against the vertical spruce and balsams, trying to see a darker patch against a dark background, trying to catch the flick of an ear against the stillness of the forest.

Nothing.

Silently I paddled to a shore opposite of where the moose had vanished. I sat still, kneeling on white pine needles, waiting for the animal's curiosity to get the best of it. Like Rudie, I felt that the moose was still there, riled that I had interrupted his breakfast.

Five minutes. Ten.

Then, from up the ridge on the opposite shore, came the sound. More than a snort this time. It was the call of a bull moose. It was a sound resonant and large, part anger and part pride. Not a cry. Not a wail. But a short, powerful bawl that seemed to hang over the bay like a spell.

That was all.

No crashing of brush. No raking of antlers. Nothing more.

The sun rose over a phalanx of spruce in the east, dripping like warm butterscotch down the cedars on the west side of the bay. It dripped down small boughs, larger boughs and trunks, spreading along the shoreline until it warmed the needles I was sitting on. It was time to go.

I picked up Furtman, and we paddled slowly down the lake one final time. I told him my tale. We were quiet for a time.

"I keep thinking, 'Well, there's always next year,'" Furtman said. "But there isn't a next year."

There's 1997. If we're lucky.

City Trees

I have been out walking, looking at trees. Not out in the woods. Right here in town.

It's no picnic, being a city tree. City trees tend to suffer more abuse then their rural relatives. The abuse isn't malicious, of course, but it's there just the same.

I was thinking, on my tree walk, about something that happened a few weeks ago. It was a fine fall day, and a friend and I were walking to lunch. We were in downtown Duluth, walking along one of our spiffy brick sidewalks next to a spiffy brick street. The sidewalk was lined with trees — the trees that were planted along with the bricking project.

My buddy, a fellow who's usually sensitive to the natural world, reached up and plucked a leaf from a tree. We kept walking. We passed another tree, and he ripped down another leaf. I couldn't figure it. I asked him why he kept ripping leaves off the trees. He said he just wanted to see how far along the leaves were toward falling.

It's no picnic, being a city tree.

On my walk I studied Duluth's downtown trees. I am ashamed to say I don't know for sure what kind they are. I know most of my woods trees, but these city trees were some decorative jobs, no doubt specified by landscape architects the world over whenever some city decides to "streetscape" its downtown.

You can't just plant a tree along a downtown street. Nope. You've got to cover the dirt where it grows with iron grates. Or gird the tree up to branch level with wrought iron. Or put it in a concrete planter.

Many of our city trees come complete with their own electrical power boxes that juice up the little light bulbs strung through the trees all year long.

The trees were bare of leaves now, this being November. But their girded bases were adorned with the debris of a populace on the move.

A Marlboro package. A Styrofoam cup. An election flyer telling us that we should vote for an enlightened candidate.

The debris was caught in the wrought iron or stuffed into the dirt, captive until the next northeaster rifles through downtown.

Cigarette butts. A McDonald's coffee cup. A Copenhagen snuff tin.

For the most part, the trees themselves appeared to be in good shape. If someone had plucked their leaves, it was no matter now. I noticed only a couple of broken branches, which isn't bad for several blocks of city trees.

Lights weren't the only things strung in the trees, however. A couple of them, near a hotel, wore drapings of toilet paper. Another, near a bank, was tinseled with the innards of a cassette tape.

Litter is one thing: You can find litter anywhere in a city. I found myself wondering about trees living in the shadow of a 12-story building. And what about the roots? Just where do they go? Is there room for them down there amid the sewer pipes and water lines and gas mains?

I wondered about those things as I walked.

I thought about other city trees. Those in city parks and along residential streets probably have a good go of it, although I'm not so sure the same is true for those that breathe a lot of exhaust along busy streets. I feel especially sorry for power-line trees — the ones that wear their crowns in a kind of reverse mohawk haircut so they won't obstruct power lines.

And that's to say nothing of trees that have been spindled and pocked by the nails of house address numerals, reflective markers and countless rummage-sale posters.

The alternative would be not to have city trees, and I'm not ready for that. If we had no city trees, there would be no shade along the avenues. I can think of wet fall days when the most memorable part of my day was seeing rows of maple trees with their rain-darkened trunks and their shouting colors. And I'll admit it. I think those Christmas lights on the trees downtown put some silent sparkle into December evenings.

I kept walking. Green gum. Red gum. A lollipop stick. A music magazine. An empty pint of Windsor Canadian whiskey. A chocolate milk carton.

It's no picnic being a city tree.

Pheasant at Sunset

The pheasant hunter slipped out of the car quietly. He squeezed the door shut behind him.

Pheasant hunters always squeeze their car doors shut. They know that too much clicking of metal makes rooster pheasants nervous. Nervous roosters rarely flush within gun range.

The hunter was heavy with anticipation. He wasn't sure why. He'd hunted this little patch three times already this season without putting a bird up.

This time was different. The sun was setting.

Something happens to this hunter at sunset. Something he can't exactly describe. Something he just feels inside.

He has talked to other hunters about it. They feel it, too, they say. They can't describe it either.

Senses seem supercharged. The natural world seems intensely alive. Adrenalin seems to flow for no apparent reason.

This doesn't happen just in the waning moments of daylight. If you have paddled a canoe at dawn on a wilderness lake, you know the feeling. If you've waded into a trout stream at first light, you understand.

At those times, too, the spell is cast. It doesn't last long, but the magic returns once again, just before dusk.

The hunter slipped into the weeds. They were thigh-high and thick. A pheasant haven. Bordered by soybeans on one side and milo stubble on the other. A pheasant smorgasbord.

The bird was up. It caught the hunter leaning too far forward, but he brought the gun up instinctively.

Already his mind was processing the information his eyes were sending. Color — splashes of it. Something red. A ring of white. Deep, dark browns.

Instantly his mind printed out the verification — rooster — and gave his trigger finger the go-ahead.

His first shot tipped the bird, but that was all. The hunter wasn't surprised because he'd felt as if he was falling down when he shot. Already his mind was reading the messages sent up by the legs and had the problem corrected.

A second shot dropped the bird, and it disappeared behind a small rise, out of sight.

The rise turned out to be a creek bank, and the hunter, in his haste to get to the bird, found himself in the bottom of the gully, knees and elbows resting on frozen mud.

Up again, over the other bank, trying to keep a line on the bird. He rushed to where he thought the bird might be. More weeds. Knee-high. Much cover for a wounded pheasant.

Then the hunter's eye caught a drop of blood on a blade of grass. And a breast feather. The hunter froze, hoping desperately the bird would make a move and reveal itself.

Ten seconds. Twenty seconds. He dropped his cap to mark the spot. Thirty seconds.

Then he heard it. The buffeting of wings against dry weeds. He let his ears guide his eyes to the bird, hunkered in short grass at the edge of the cover. Alive.

Quietly the hunter eased closer. He knelt down. The rooster was beautiful. It blinked.

The hunter does not remember seeing his hand grab the bird. Suddenly he was holding it. He wrung the bird's neck to kill it. Quickly. He didn't like doing it.

He remained kneeling, shotgun across his lap, looking at the bird. He turned it slowly in his hand, watching the sunlight play on the iridescence of its feathers. He felt the bird's warmth.

He isn't sure how long he knelt there, looking at the bird.

When he looked up the sun was gone.

Winter

Winter Comes
Hero Trips
Pyropiscathon
Away from the Crowd
Superior Shore

Moving Pictures

Winter Comes

It was the kind of day that made car exhaust pipes look like dragon nostrils. They weren't exhaling so much as snorting. It was cold.

Just how cold depended on where your thermometer was being read. If you lived in the hinterlands, yours might have read 30 below zero.

With a northwest wind whistling at 15 miles per hour, the wind chill was somewhere between 60 and 70 below.

Just before sunrise I cruised through town. I knew I wanted to be out early on this first cool day of winter.

On street corners, school kids put their backs to the wind and waited for school buses. Grade-schoolers had popped up on curbs like little red mushrooms. They were ensconced in their snowsuits, swaddled in scarfs, drawn into their hoods. All you could see were their eyes. They looked happy. They were bouncing around, leaning into each other with their bulky little bodies. They wouldn't have known it was cold unless their parents had made such a fuss cinching them up before sending them out the door.

Then there were the junior and senior high students. These are good kids, but at that age strange hormones are surging through their veins. One of those hormones is the one that prevents them from wearing hats, gloves or thick jackets. We all suffered from the same hormonal imbalance. We've just forgotten about it. The junior and senior high kids stood on the curbs like Popsicle sticks. They didn't look happy. But their hair looked good, which is all that mattered.

I wasn't cruising town to check out school kids, though. I wanted to see the lake.

It is something, living in a place that gives you 30 below zero and a lake that won't freeze. When the two get together, unusual things happen. I caught my first glimpse while still high on the hill. Fog — a solid bank of it — rising above the pines, filling up the sky where normally I would look across the lake and see the town of Superior.

I had planned to drive straight down to the lakeshore to get a closer look, but I pulled off at an overlook. Lake Superior was nowhere to be seen. It was blanketed with a comforter of fog. The lake was a cauldron of soup set out on a giant back porch to cool.

The fog stretched as far as I could see toward Two Harbors and Grand Marais. It seemed thinner there and thickest where the lake tucked itself into the harbors of Duluth and Superior. Thick and gray and alive.

It moved slowly in great, undulating lumps of vapor. It was hard to tell how thick the blanket was at the Duluth end. A hundred feet at least. Maybe two hundred or three hundred feet.

A brown pickup pulled up nearby. The driver got out. He was on his way to work, he said. He stood there in a blue parka and red stocking cap, just looking.

"I had to come up and check this out," he said.

He had lived all of his 28 years in Duluth, and still he couldn't let a morning like this slip by without a close inspection. He isn't one to let opportunities pass. He and a friend had celebrated part of New Year's Eve with a quick dip in Lake Superior.

"Five seconds at the most," he said.

Now, here in the new year, he let his gaze ride down the shore from northeast to southwest, looking at the fog swirl and glide, contemplating life in the grip of a northern winter at the edge of this superior lake.

"This is something else," he said finally.

He was right, of course.

We stood there a few minutes longer. Then we each crawled back into our cocoons of warmth and drove off to work.

Hero Trips

We should be able to see the sun by now. But we don't. Not on this February morning.

As night and day wrestle for control of the next ten hours, the three of us ski north — Dan and Jeff and me. We are skiing the lakes from Minnesota to Canada.

Our skis hiss. My bindings squeak with each stride. I can already feel my pack pulling on my shoulders.

This is a little crazy. We are, I think, defining the limits of a day fishing trip. We will ski about eight miles on four lakes, then shed our skis and walk another mile or so into the destination lake.

Nine miles one way. Three hours if the going's good.

Then we'll fish for four hours and ski out.

Eighteen miles under packs — packs that will be heavier on the way home, if the lake trout cooperate.

Dan and Jeff have done this sort of thing a few times already this winter. "Hero trips," Jeff calls them.

Some folks would say it's foolish to spend six hours skiing and walking, all for only four hours of fishing. I happen to think four hours is about the right amount of time to dangle a line through a hole in the ice.

The otters must wonder at these upright intruders sliding along the ice. Two of the animals are cavorting at the edge of some open water below a set of falls. In the distance they look like short black humps. Silently, I wonder how many more fish they'll catch during the day than we will.

We switch leads often, sharing the work of breaking trail. The snow is crusted and easy going in some spots, deep and sugary in others. It is also pure and white and untouched. I think of the snow I've left behind in the city. Snow doesn't have much to say about where it falls, I suppose, but if I were a snowflake, I'd prefer the woods.

The mile-long portage delivers us to the lake. We pause on the shore, drinking in the lake's whiteness. Then we drill six holes and get down to business. A snow-squall whips up and drives big flakes horizontally against the backdrop of jackpines and balsam firs.

The temperature is probably in the teens, but the wind won't let us enjoy it.

"Pretty cold for a warm day, isn't it?" Dan says.

Down some holes we dangle dead and semi-frozen ciscoes. Through other holes we jig lures called Swedish Pimples and Krocodiles with cisco tails impaled on their hooks.

By lunchtime we have two fish on the ice. The fish are products of the dangling ciscoes. Each lake trout takes the bait in customary lake-trout fashion, grabbing the cisco and swimming away with it. We let the lines free-spool out, watching like little kids as the spools pay out line.

After its initial run the lake trout stops. Now he'll swallow the cisco, and with it the hook. How a lake trout can ingest a baitfish and not notice a treble hook has always amazed me, but it happens.

Then the unknowing lake trout swims on, the hook in his belly. That's when the angler standing on top of two feet of ice begins pulling up his line. The fish doesn't fight hard, not nearly as hard as if hooked in the lip. It's a lot easier, I suppose, to shake your head from side to side than your stomach.

The fish come up through the hole cold and firm and wide-eyed. We marvel at their color, their dark gray sides and their creamy spots. Then we kick a slot in the snow, slide the fish in and kick snow over them.

Back in the woods where the wind can't find us, we toast peanut-butter sandwiches and heat hot-chocolate water over a small fire. Jeff makes soup from two packages of noodles.

The fire is significant. Not only does it boil our soup and hot-drink water, it somehow symbolizes the simple trail life. It seems to stand for self-reliance and getting by on your own in the woods. In this highly technological world, a fire is the old-fashioned, simple way to get warm and to cook food. It works.

It burns down through the snow, exposing duff and needles and leaves, reminding us of seasons past.

After lunch, we catch six more fish. A four-pounder, an almost-four-pounder, a two-and-a-half-pounder and three smaller but keepable lakers. They all come in a quick streak, and we rush about the ice from one angler's hole to another in a fishing frenzy.

We help each other land fish. We help each other remove hooks. We cheer each other's efforts.

We are having some fun now. But we keep an eye on the watch.

At 2:30 we load packs, adding the 15 pounds of lake trout we've pulled through the ice.

The going is slow. Dan is hobbled by a sore knee. He

has an appointment for arthroscopic surgery in five days.

We walk the portage and ski past the otters. We make another portage. We try to find the trail we've skied in on, but the snowstorm and wind have all but erased it.

Darkness and daylight begin wrestling again, and this time darkness wins. The remnant trail disappears. We are still five miles from our starting point.

Now we are shuffling through the deep sugar again, playing a frustrating mind game: Do we try to find the old trail and stay on it, or simply trudge on in the deep stuff?

We trudge. Occasionally, we stumble onto our old trail. We ski almost effortlessly for a few strides, only to lose the trail again.

We talk less and less, choosing to concentrate on the task at hand. Now it is fully dark. We stop for snacks twice. We fantasize about the potluck supper that awaits us.

I am somewhat light-headed. Jeff says he feels as if he were floating. Dan says he feels good, except for his knee.

Finally we see lights near the landing. Still, it takes us half an hour to get there. It is almost seven p.m. when we arrive.

We are spent, warm, happy, wet. And, though no one says it, maybe a little relieved.

"These trips are good," Jeff says, "about once a month."

Pyropiscathon

Occasionally on winter fishing trips I get to thinking about an old idea of mine, a brilliant idea.

I'll be thinking about how cold my lips are and how good it would be to build a fire. I would fish, of course, but boiling some tea water around that fire would be a significant part of the day. Maybe the most significant.

That's when I get to thinking about my idea for a new Winter Olympics event — the pyropiscathon. Pyro, meaning fire. Pisca, meaning fish. Thon, meaning anything that takes a long time to do and involves sweat, lactic acid and the possibility of blisters.

In order to be an Olympic pyropiscathlete, one would cross-country ski five or six miles into a little trout lake, build a fire, boil up a pot of tea, catch a fish and ski back out.

One of the best things the pyropiscathon has going for it is that participants don't have to wear those skin-tight suits that the downhill skiers and luge competitors wear. Some of those people look as if they were standing naked somewhere when someone threw a bucket of peppermint paint at them.

All you need for the pyropiscathon is a good pair of wool pants, a couple of wool shirts, a pair of knock-around skis, a fire-blackened tea pot and a stubby fishing rod.

The event would be open to men and women, which only makes sense, because once you get all those clothes on, it's hard to tell the men from the women anyway. It also makes it easier to judge the East Germans.

The event would begin with a mass start in which hundreds of participants would try to back pickup trucks into small parking lots that haven't been plowed all winter.

Then the skiing would begin. Once at the designated lake, the competitors would drill fishing holes and begin building fires.

We'd have to get some crusty guide to do commentary on the fire-building portion, which would be judged by a panel of snooty-looking people trained to hold up numbered cards while displaying no other visible sign of life.

Style points for fire building would account for only 20 percent of a competitor's overall score. Raw time counts for a lot, so the angler who catches the first fish still — as always — gets the glory.

As I see it, the pyropiscathon has everything — speed, stamina, finesse. And it has one more thing most Olympic events lack. When you retire from a successful career as a pyropiscathlete, you don't go back home wondering what to do.

You just keep on doing it.

Away from the Crowd

Jim Hawk's breath hung in the night air like lazy thoughts. You could see them well in the beam of his headlamp, condensed vaporlets of words that congealed in paragraph-sized clouds before they finally drifted into the alders.

The 1988 John Beargrease Sled Dog Marathon had begun, but all was quiet at Hawk's haunt here on the outskirts of Duluth. Hawk was staffing a tricky corner and bridge crossing about six miles into the race.

He was supported by his friends Mary and Sheila Hansen, a thermos of coffee and a supply of crackers and cheese.

It was just the four of us — and the humble fire Hawk had built.

All was dark, except for the lithium-powered beam of Hawk's headlamp and the blinking of an orange hazard light near the bridge. The only sounds were brittle boots on subzero snow and the occasional hum of a car on a nearby road. The only smell was campfire smoke.

In short, it was going to be a good place to watch a dogsled race unfold. Noticeably absent were the hype and howl of the starting-line scene, the bawling of dogs crazy to run and the Alaskan look of mushers suiting up for a chilly night on the trail.

"I stood at the start for two years," Mary Hansen was saying. "That's definitely where you get the adrenalin."

She's right. That's what hooks you on this 470-mile spectacle of dogspeed, this race to Grand Portage and back. But after you have watched 29 teams quit barking and bolt from the starting chute, you can't help but wonder what it's like out there, under the stars on that ribbon of snow called the North Shore Trail.

"Can you imagine going down a trail like this for hours and hours and nobody on it?" Sheila Hansen said.

Those are the kind of thoughts that vaporize in front of you on a lonely corner of trail when every hair outside your face mask turns white with frost.

The snowmobile caravan came through first, 22 one-eyed thoraxes that together looked like a punk-rock serpent. Their blue belchings had just about wafted away when a lonely headlamp appeared through the aspens.

It was Brad Pozarnsky, the first musher. Unlike the snowmachines, Pozarnsky's team came almost silently. If you watched only the headlamp, you were startled by the quick appearance of the lead dogs ahead of it. That's how long a string of 16 or 18 dogs is.

They were trotting fast, tongues adangle, eyes bright and searching. They ran through a cloud of their own breath that made the glow of Pozarnsky's headlamp larger than it should have been.

The only sounds were the panting and the hiss of sled runners, like pushing a knife across polyester. That was all. The lead dogs found the corner, centered the team

on the bridge and hustled on. Pozarnsky danced the
sled around a bale of hay. They were gone.

They came by the kennelfuls after that.

Bill Gallea of Grand Marais. Jamie Nelson of Togo.
John Suter and his poodle-husky team. You had to look
twice to see the poodles through all the breath. They
just looked like more sled dogs.

Some drivers gave their dogs a "gee" — musher talk for
a right turn — to get them around the corner. Some let
the dogs find it on their own. Several thanked the trail
crew.

"Mushers are the nicest people," Mary Hansen said.

They kept coming. Ed Dallas, who had been the first
musher to start, came through running fourteenth.
Then Alaska's Eric Buetow. Another came, talking to
his team: "Good girls. Good girls. Gee."

Eyes. Always it was the eyes you saw first, after the
headlamp. Dog eyes. Chartreuse holes in the night.

Then it was feet. Dog feet — forty-eight or sixty-four
or seventy-two, flicking from the wrist down, seeming
almost not to touch the ground before they were up
again, and the little flick was repeated.

Then came the growing glow of the musher's headlamp, illuminating that low cloud of breath. Then a bib
number, a quick look at a snowy backside, and — *hiss*
— the night swallowed them again.

Twenty-nine of them. Twenty-nine that seemed like
about twelve, and you had to go home when you were
just getting used to the cold and you'd poured yourself
a cup of tea and you'd found Orion reclining in the sky
looking down on the whole works.

The Beargrease was only an hour or so old. We
would go home and sleep. Twenty-nine teams would
trot through the night.

Can you imagine going down a trail like that for hours and hours and nobody on it?

Yes we could, a little bit. Now that we'd seen them at this quiet corner by the bridge.

Superior Shore

The last time I had come to this beach, brown bodies slathered with suntan oil were lying everywhere.

Now, on this afternoon in midwinter, I was alone. Alone with the ice.

I had had a hunch it might be a good day to make an ice inspection. The day was even better than I had figured.

This beach is just a wide spot in the sandspit that is Minnesota Point, which extends six miles from the Duluth Ship Canal toward Wisconsin. The sliver of sand separates Lake Superior from the Duluth-Superior harbor, and along its eastern edge it catches anything the big lake sends it.

In summer that might be driftwood or ladybugs. In mid-January it's ice.

I walked out on the frozen sand. A long strip of landfast ice, about as wide as a logging road, clung to the shore for the length of the beach. Beyond that lay a slurry of ice water that rose and fell with the big lake's breathing.

The slurry was composed of ice particles of all sizes. There were tiny shards, ice-cube sized and smaller. There were fist-size chunks of ice. There were flat pans that ranged in size from manhole covers to car hoods. There were filing cabinet icebergs. And there were the unmoving islands of ice as large as two semitrailer trucks. The ice islands were one hundred yards from shore, grounded on the sand bottom.

I stood in pleasant awe, gripped by the immensity of the spectacle before me. At first the sensation was purely visual, the gentle movement of those tons of ice, heaving and dipping with each incoming roller. It was a slithering mass that neutralized the full effect of every wave long before it could reach shore.

Watching the waves move through the ice was like watching cats crawling beneath a comforter.

But I realized that watching the ice was only half the show. Listening to it was equally stimulating. Early on I sensed only a constant rustle. Then I closed my eyes. Sometimes you have to close your eyes to hear something right. I listened again, and it came to me that the rustling was the sum of a million tiny tinklings.

It sounded like someone walking along bearing a huge tray loaded with glasses of iced tea.

I moved on down the beach, and I could see I wasn't the only one who had witnessed this ice show. The wet sand was just loose enough to accept shallow footprints, and there were many of them.

After walking the beach for a while, I wanted to get closer to the undulating ice. I took hesitating steps onto the shorefast ice. What's the worst that could happen, I asked myself. If I broke through, the water would surely be no deeper than a foot or two.

I ventured farther out, until I was near the lip of the shelf ice, and I could study the moving ice more thoroughly. Out on the lake, in a strip of open water, the waves looked like about one-footers. They remained one-footers through the first 20 yards of slurry. They lifted all the little icelings, and even some of the berglets.

By the time the waves had penetrated half the slurry, they had lost their energy. It had been absorbed by the ice itself. By the time a wave reached the foot of the shelf ice where I was standing, all it could muster was a minor heave and a slow, sideways jostle.

I walked on down the shelf ice. A lone herring gull flew over, looking clean against a sky the color of escalator steps.

When you are standing on its shore, Lake Superior always looks big. But it doesn't always make you feel small. That's how the ice show made me feel. Little. Insignificant.

A good surf rolling in will do the same thing. Or an outboard motor that won't start when you're a couple of miles out. And now, the ice.

I wouldn't want to feel that way all the time. But I don't mind being reminded of my scale in this world once in a while.

Moving Pictures

I'll tell you why we came here. We came here, Phyllis
and I, because we saw the pictures in the brochures. In
the pictures, the lakes were blue. That might not sound
like much, but when you've grown up where all the
lakes are brown with cornfield runoff, you almost
wonder if the photos from Up North have been
retouched.

In the pictures, men were holding up toothy northern
pike and bug-eyed walleyes and broad bass.

In the pictures, someone in a red shirt was tending a
griddle full of fish fillets over a campfire.

That's what got us here. And the brochure, from an
Ely canoe outfitter, came in an envelope designed as a
Duluth pack. That was all it took.

At first it was just a September canoe trip. A week
Up North. I'll tell you how green we were. On Knife
Lake, up on the Canadian border, we thought the wail-
ing of loons was the howling of timberwolves. We
thought reeds in the shallows were shafts of wild rice.
We had trouble making a fire on a damp morning.

But the North had taken us in. The water really was blue. And you could drink it in drippy handfuls right from the canoe.

So, a couple of years later, we moved north. I can still remember driving the forest road down to Moose Lake near Ely that May afternoon, pulling the little U-Haul trailer with the few possessions we considered essential. I can remember seeing Moose Lake gleaming through the new birch leaves. It might as well have been a picture in a brochure. It was blue.

Working for a canoe outfitter, we came to know the woods that summer. We packed Duluth packs and hung tents out to dry and listened to the stories of those who came back from the woods.

We learned birds and blueberries and bears. We learned loons and lakes and layover days.

But we never planned to stay. We figured a year, maybe. We'd saved some money. We could get by.

A lot of people come north with that sort of plan. A week. A summer. A year. They're still here, too. The North has taken them in, just as it did us.

It has been twelve years now since that first summer on Moose Lake. The roots are going deeper. We build fires in the rain now. We have heard the timberwolves. We have caught some of those northern pike and walleyes.

But if that were all that mattered, we could do it from Minneapolis or Des Moines or Kansas City. What has kept us here, I think, is all of the little events that string together all the big ones. The little seasons. The small moments. The intangibles.

We have come to know the feeling you get for a Duluth pack that you've paddled and portaged with for a few hundred miles.

We have known the quiet of a morning camp when

the mist is rising from the water like spirits from the past.

We have seen the first ice forming in the fall and felt the grip of another winter coming on.

It is all woven together now — the bird sounds, the forest smells, the anticipations of the coming season. Now we know to go no matter what the weather will be and that, likely as not, we'll come across some small event worth remembering. We know that it's worth it even in blackfly season and in the depth of winter or before the aspens have leafed out in spring.

The North is rich with the glories of life. Sometimes you have to poke your nose in the dirt, and sometimes you have to muck around in the swamps and sometimes you have to get up with the geese.

But it's there, awaiting discovery.

The pictures in the brochures tried to tell us that. Little did we know it was so much better than they led us to believe.

Other titles by Sam Cook

Up North

CampSights

If This is Mid-Life, Where's the Crisis?

 Pfeifer-Hamilton Publishers
210 West Michigan
Duluth MN 55802-1908
218-727-0500